LITTLE PATUXENT REVIEW

Copyright © 2021 LPR Enterprises, Inc., a nonprofit corporation.
Little Patuxent Review (ISSN: 1941-2053) is published biannually
by LPR Enterprises, Inc., in Columbia, Maryland.

Logo design by Kristen Powell

Publisher:
Kellyn Mahan

Publisher Emeritus:
Michael J. Clark

General Manager:
Phyllis Greenbaum

Editor:
Chelsea Lemon Fetzer

Poetry Editor:	*Fiction Editor:*	*Nonfiction Editor:*
Evan Lesavoy	Lisa Lynn Biggar	Dominique Cahn
Design Editor:	*Online Editor:*	
David Saunier	Holly Bowers	
Videographer:	*Art Consultant:*	
Alan King	Abdu Mongo Ali	

Contributing Editors:
Susan Thornton Hobby, Ann Bracken, Abdu Mongo Ali

Copy Editor:
Kellie Hagan

Review Committee:
Linda Joy Burke, Dan Crawley, Shelby Harper, Raima Larter, Russell Reece, Emily Rich, Jessica Sullivan, Andy Weaver

Board of Directors:
Elizabeth Bobo, George Clack, Michael J. Clark, Alex Duvan, Brian England, Willie Flowers, Phyllis Greenbaum, Debbie Jaskulek, Elizabeth Mason Moses

Address:
Little Patuxent Review
PO Box 6084
Columbia, MD 21045

Logo design by Kristen Powell

Website: www.littlepatuxentreview.org
Contact: editor@littlepatuxentreview.org
Submissions: littlepatuxentreview.submittable.com/submit
Twitter: @LPReview
Facebook: facebook.com/LittlePatuxentReview
Instagram: instagram.com/littlepatuxentreview/

Acknowledgments

Thanks to the following institutions for their support: the Howard County Arts Council, the Howard County Government, the Maryland State Arts Council, the National Endowment for the Arts, Community Foundation of Howard County, and individual contributors for their financial support, as well as HoCoPoLitSo for its assistance.

Little Patuxent Review is supported by grants from Howard County Arts Council and the Maryland State Arts Council, an agency dedicated to cultivating a vibrant cultural community where the arts thrive. Funding for the Maryland State Arts Council is also provided by the National Endowment for the Arts, a federal agency, which believes that a great nation deserves great art.

Maryland State Arts Council

"Tomato Pies, 25 Cents" by Grace Cavalieri, from *Sounds Like Something I Would Say*, 2010, Casa Menendez Press. "How a Poem Begins" by Grace Cavalieri, from *Water On The Sun*, 2006, Bordighera Press. "Safety" by Grace Cavalieri, from *Other Voices, Other Lives*, 2017, Alan Squire Pub. "This Poem is Asking for Your Love" by Grace Cavalieri, from *What The Psychic Said*, 2020, Goss 183 Pub. "Haberdashery" by Grace Cavalieri, from *The Man Who Got Away*, 2014, New Academia/Scarif. All poems reprinted by permission of the author.

Little Patuxent Review is the rebirth of a literary magazine originally published in the late 1970s. The renewal of publication serves as a living memorial to the late Ralph and Margot Treitel, Columbia, Maryland, poets who founded the original run of the publication. *Little Patuxent Review* strives to promote the tradition of written and visual arts by creating a spirited magazine that reflects and draws upon the creativity and diversity within Howard County, the region, and the nation.

On the Cover
Heavy is the Head, 2020
s.e.a.
Digital Image

Contents

POETRY

LIZ HOLLAND	*7-Year-Old in a Polka Dot Jumper*	6
SARAH B. SULLIVAN	*A Reckoning*	10
DAVID BERGMAN	*The Man Who Could Carry a Tune*	11
BRIAN WALLACE BAKER	*Holding Sunlight*	42
ELYSE THOMAS	*Vignette of a Puerto Rican Summer*	43
ALYSSA CRUZ	*Bedhog*	62
EVAN WILLIAMS	*Something Quite Big*	63
SOPHIA TARIN	*The Mute Button*	64
MISCHELLE ANTHONY	*The Heart is Difficult to Know*	75
CATHERINE-ESTHER COWIE	*Still Singing Even Without Faith in the Universe*	76
KRISTIN KOWALSKI FERRAGUT	*Underneath Quarantine*	91
GRACE CAVALIERI	*How a Poem Begins*	100
	This Poem is Asking For Your Love	101
	Safety	102
	Tomato Pies, 25 Cents	103
	Haberdashery	104
ROBERT L. PENICK	*Duty*	110
SUSAN JOHNSON	*Crumbs*	111

FICTION

JIHOON PARK	*The Suspended Boulder*	13
KATHLEEN WHEATON	*Visitation*	29
PETE FORTENBAUGH	*Inheritance*	67
BRIANA MALEY	*Hummingbird*	79

ESSAY/NON-FICTION

MARY BETH STULLER	The Blurred Lines of Work/Life and the Beagle That Binds Them	7
RACHELE SALVINI	Stellar	38
MADISON DURAND	Brave Iguana People Only Love Acid Rain	65
ELIZABETH FELICETTI	Armed	82
KAREN KORETSKY	Supermoon	105

INTERVIEWS

SUSAN THORNTON HOBBY	An Interview with Gish Jen	20
ABDU MONGO ALI	A Conversation with Featured Artist s.e.a.	44
ANN BRACKEN	An Interview with Grace Cavalieri	92

CONTRIBUTORS' NOTES   113

Editor's Note

In their daytime pajamas, aka *we-aren't-going-anywhere-again* clothes, my little daughters have adapted their adventure hunts, rerouting to the tuckaways and forgotten bottom drawers in our house. In an old desk, they uncovered the treasure that beat all: a box of looking lenses, red, blue, yellow. They held them up to their eyes: one color, two colors combined . . . they found each other through them. Then, they rediscovered my wife, me—red, blue, yellow, and all the possible in-betweens.

This issue was compiled in a divisive political time for our country, and we have now spent most of a year isolated, social distancing, and grieving due to the COVID pandemic. LPR did not call for any theme in our submissions, and the variety of work herein explores far more than this moment. Yet, as I read these selections, it strikes me they are a bright collection of lenses too. Uncovered just now. They offer so many colors through which we might relook, and even play, at what connection could mean—at being human. How would an early love be revisited with a fever, for example? And why might a musical duo depend on a boulder? What could an old figurine sitting on the desk beside your Zoom class reveal about family? Can a hummingbird change the color of grief?

Our featured artist, s.e.a., and Baltimore-based performing artist, Abdu Mongo Ali, examine radical joy in queer BIPOC communities and a quarantine-inspired project connecting afro-futurism with a scavenger hunt for nature in Brooklyn, New York. In our interviews, we hear from the novelist Gish Jen on writing America as a child of Chinese immigrants. Maryland's own poet laureate, Grace Cavalieri, divulges her preference between radio and Zoom.

I was so honored when Steven Leyva asked me if I would like to take the helm as editor of *Little Patuxent Review*, a journal I have long admired as a writer and a reader. This issue is my first, and it has been a perfect inspiration.

7-year-old in a Polka-Dot Jumper

Like how the one yellow peony blooms
in the middle of a storm. Like how the fence
can't keep the mint from throwing itself
across the grass. Like how bubbles when split,
still float on complete. Like how trees, when
struck by lightning, become two trees. Like
how grapes gather in death only to breathe life
into wine. Like how even the smallest ant can
carry an army of itself. Like how this wholeness
has never been disturbed. Like how the body
replaces itself on a seven-year cell cycle. Like
how mosaics remain perfect up close. Like how
you leap into the air not knowing if the ground
will catch you. Like how you will learn to catch
you.

MARY BETH STULLER

The Blurred Lines of Work/Life and the Beagle That Binds Them

For my students at Hereford High School

A tiny ceramic beagle stands on my desk, beside the laptop screen, and looks at me as I look at you, framed in your bedroom squares. It measures two inches, nose to tail, and its glossy coat reflects the window light. A whimsical thing for a woman to have, it's a gift from my grandmother, long dead now. We called her Dooda, a name my sister babbled, and it stuck.

Dooda lived in Ventnor City, a coastal town in South Jersey. Its streets, in grids that connect it to Atlantic City to the north and Margate and Longport to the south, are the same streets that populate a Monopoly board. From her house, I crossed Ventnor and Atlantic avenues to get to the beach.

My family never went on vacations; we'd go visit Dooda—two blocks from the ocean. This was before Airbnbs, and weekly rentals were not allowed there. Dooda looked down at renters who booked houses for summer. Each year she complained, "Another family from Philadelphia to use our beach and leave . . ." Ventnor was a residential town, and that's how she liked it. Envious of my friends who vacationed in tourist-tacky Ocean City, Maryland, where aqua-hued motels lined Coastal Highway, I spent late afternoons riding my aunt's old bike down the edged sidewalks of Ventnor, past blue hydrangeas that anchored porch fronts.

Sometimes my parents would take me, their youngest, to Ocean City, New Jersey, where the boardwalk featured amusement rides and junk shops. The nighttime trek over the Longport/Ocean City Bridge revealed a kaleidoscope of colored lights, their reflection on the water doubly enticing. There's a scene in The Great Gatsby when Jay drives Nick Carraway in the yellow coupe from Long Island to Manhattan. Nick says, "The city seen from the Queensboro Bridge is always the city seen for the first time, in its first wild promise of all the mystery and the beauty of the world." That's how I felt as a kid in the backseat of my dad's Toyota, watching the lights full of promise, the electric beauty of childhood.

On at least one trip I must've cried over a disappointment. A dropped cone? An overthrown ring-toss? But mostly, I remember riding the Tilt-a-Whirl with my dad. The two of us. The centrifugal force pulling us together. In a family with seven kids, alone time with Dad was a big deal. He's dead now, too.

After the Tilt-a-Whirl, we strolled the boards, and this is where Dooda bought me my little beagle in a shop full of knick-knacks and decaled souvenirs. A menagerie of animals stood silent on shelves, their feet secured to manila-colored squares, a price scrawled in the corner.

In the olden days, when people shopped used bookstores and leafed through musty pages grabbed from dusty shelves, they'd handle the tomes with germy fingers and breathe the stale air in cramped aisles, content to slip in and out of novels, histories, art. Some customers leaned on tables stacked with merchandise; others squatted before low shelves; the nimble and committed sat cross-legged on the floor. And inside the cover of each book was written the cost in a sure but hurried hand. That's how the price appeared on this beagle's placard—a large two—and then fifty a bit smaller, underscored with a lead stripe.

Dooda bought me this token to remember my visit and because I loved beagles. I longed for a dog but was denied any pet. It was the '70s and, with nine mouths to feed, my parents had no money for nonhumans. The instant Carnation milk—its powder clumped in my glass—was proof enough.

Beagles were adorable, with big eyes and long, perky ears, and unlike a lab they were smaller than me when they jumped in greeting. A neighbor's grown son owned one. Whenever the son came to visit, I entertained the dog. We played fetch and tug of war, and when the dog tired I sat in the grass and pet her suede-soft ears. I vowed when I grew up, I'd get a beagle of my own.

The day my husband and I settled on our first home, we drove to the breeder and picked up the beagle puppy who'd been waiting for us. We named her Dempsey, and she loved our attention. Every night my husband lobbed balls for her, and I'd rub her tummy when she reclined in my lap. After our son was born, she'd sit beside his carrier or, later, his high chair and lick the sticky fingers he willingly put in her mouth. She even let him rest his head on her side as they lounged in a panel of sunlight.

But when we left the house, Dempsey rebelled. She'd chew up toys and mess the floor. We took her out constantly, afraid of more accidents, and she'd tug the leash till it hurt—as if all she wanted was freedom. A couple times when my husband clipped her nails, she bared her teeth. We wondered what might provoke her to bite. A toddler's tug of a tail? Once our daughter arrived, Dempsey's behavior got worse.

One day, as I played on the floor with the children, Dempsey up and died. She convulsed, her tongue lolling out of her mouth, then nothing.

When my husband came home, I told him, "Dempsey's dead."
"Why? What'd she do this time?"
"No, I mean she's not alive anymore."
He beamed.
Funny how dreams play out.

And still I have this beagle from Dooda that traveled from house to house. I found it in a tiny box when I reorganized my home office for the new school year. A lot of people have home offices, but I waited decades to get what Virginia Woolf called "a room of one's own."

As a kid I shared a room with two sisters. Once they moved out, my private space morphed into a hamper, a place to dump clothes as I hustled from school to practice to work. College, marriage, and babies soon occupied my life and left little time for sleep, let alone privacy.

Once the nest emptied—twenty-some years later—I created a room full of pictures and posters, cards and mementos, books shelved and stacked, and it's meant to be my place to write and read and contemplate.

But now, crammed in the space, stands a stout bookcase packed with binders from school, their spines labeled with units: Hamlet, Jane Eyre, College Application Essays. It had taken me years to learn to leave work at school, that papers lugged home and plopped on the mudroom bench would get lugged back ungraded. The guilt of those papers ruined my nights from September to June. Finally, with no kids to shuttle to practice or rehearsals, I stayed at school—as long as I could bear, longer than some of you stayed for sports practice— and came home unburdened. The evening became mine to write.

Since home is now my workplace, the diptych I created of a work/life balance has smudged. "The colours have run," as Woolf would say.

And my desk—once my writing sanctuary—is now my classroom, cluttered with lesson plans and Post-it notes—even a second computer. And Dooda's beagle. A gift I'd never have told you about—never written about—in a nonpandemic world.

SARAH B. SULLIVAN

A Reckoning

Let me not forget, I cannot fix sinks.
I could never fix sinks
so I have not gone backwards.
There's a crust of rust on the faucet.

Is sink water filthy because our faces are filthy?
When does the thickness of time amass?
To know your own hands in the mirror is easy—
lean in and touch the ridges every day.

Under the basin, after the plumber came and went,
the pipe still drips grimy water. But in a hush.
He removed the stubborn clog
with a labor of determined grunts.

There's a tinge of rust in the bucket
in the cabinet below the drain trap.
This is how it works: rust does not un-oxidize.
This vanity may be beyond repair.

DAVID BERGMAN

The Man Who Could Carry a Tune

At first it didn't seem so difficult. It was light
as a nursery rhyme or a little ditty or perhaps

an earworm that was to become a butterfly
when it hatched and could be reduced to a few

nonsense syllables, tra-la-la-la-la, something like that.
But soon it got larger and could no longer fit

in his pocket and then it grew limbs like a tree
or a baby, and it grasped his neck with its hands

and his waist with its roots and held on to his back.
That was better, but he needed a rest from the demands

of the melody. They found themselves in an empty field
plowed in a way that made it look like staff paper.

A tree like a treble clef stood in the corner.
He held in his arms the melody, which had been quietly

humming to itself, but as soon as he put it down, it started
to scream and that was even more unbearable.

He picked up the tune and rocked it back and forth.
At some point it seemed to go to sleep

and everything grew as quiet as Beethoven
when he no longer heard the applause or the booing

of the audience and needed to be turned around to see the ovation.
Yes, he had grown deaf to the exterior world

but there were new sounds to listen to in his mind,
sounds no one had heard before, and they went on and on,

not formlessly but in a form so large people couldn't
view its shape from where they were standing—like the globe

whose arc is invisible as he stands on the shore at noon
and watches for even the smallest bend in the horizon.

The Suspended Boulder

The immense boulder appeared directly over town hall, stretching all the way from Al's Furniture Warehouse to the old roller rink on McKee Boulevard. We were playing a Bach fugue in our apartment on Main Street, me on the clarinet and you on the oboe, when the entire town was covered in darkness.

"Can't be night already," I said.

"Something's blocking the sun," you said, looking out the window. The wind coming in rustled your blouse. I remember that.

We watched the news.

. . . seemingly out of nowhere. Scientists and meteorologists have no explanation for its sudden appearance. For those of you just tuning in, a gigantic boulder, almost as big as Winington itself, is currently floating over . . .

We stood outside on the street, gazing up at the bottom of the boulder. It seemed to be a dark gray color, although it was difficult to see clearly under its shadow. Soon the streets were filled with townsfolk, all of them staring up at the gigantic boulder in the sky. Hotdog vendors came out. Children ran around trying to throw old milk cartons at the boulder. People set up cameras on tripods. We overheard some people saying that the airport would probably close, since the boulder was blocking the airspace.

"Guess that means you can't go to Madrid," I said.

"We'll see," you said, smiling. "If they refund my ticket I can just go to another airport."

"But our airport has those indoor hanging gardens. You like those gardens."

"That's true. They're nice to look at."

* * *

In the beginning, the people of Winington were split into two groups. Those who left town felt the boulder would succumb to the laws of gravity at any moment and crush the entire town. Those who stayed, I think, felt there was something special about the boulder. These kinds of things, in the movies anyway, happened in New York or Tokyo or London or Cairo, not in places like Winington. Those who stayed had faith that the boulder wouldn't fall, and they walked under its immense shadow fearlessly.

People from all over the world began coming to Winington. Artists set up easels on rooftops. Scientists set up strange devices in the streets, pointing radar dishes and infrared sensors up towards the boulder. They wore hazmat suits. Some of the townsfolk asked if they should have hazmat suits as well, but the scientists said that they were probably OK. A famous acrobat from Tennessee announced he would perform a trapeze routine on the underside of the boulder. He called himself "The Great Boulderini."

Advertisers quickly took advantage of the boulder. The boulder technically didn't belong to anyone, to the best of our knowledge anyway, and since so many people were looking up at it all the time the underside of the boulder soon became the most prized advertisement space in the great state of Nevada. Large banners were hung with 300-foot PVC poles. Whenever people looked up in Winington, they had to read things like *Try Kentucky Fried Chicken's New Spicy Nugget Combo, only $5.99* and *Is Your Wife Cheating on You? Probably! Hire Private Investigator Ron Hernandez, Discretion Guaranteed* and *Miss Tang's Massage Parlor, $19.99 Tuesday Specials, No Happy Endings So Stop Asking!* and so on.

It was around this time that a camera crew took the first detailed aerial photos of the boulder from a helicopter. They were published in the *Winington Gazette*, as well as many major papers across the globe. It was bigger than we had initially guessed. Winington was barely noticeable underneath its shadow. The boulder was roughly ovular in shape. There were mountainous regions on the topside that geologists were eager to explore. There seemed to be cave systems within the boulder, which some predicted were filled with minerals unknown to humanity. There were large flatland areas of smooth rock formations that indicated possible volcanic activity.

We drove two hours out into the mountains because you wanted to see the boulder in its entirety. We hiked to one of the peaks. We brought our instruments because you wanted to play a few pieces up there.

"It's so beautiful," you said, looking through the coin-operated binoculars. You used my lucky 1962 silver quarter. "It's there for no other reason than to just be there."

"What do you want to play?" I asked, putting together my clarinet.

"I don't know."

"Handel?"

"No."

"Bach?'

"No."

"Something modern then. Shostakovich. You like Shostakovich."

"I don't want to play right now."

* * *

They built a ladder up to the boulder from the roof of the cat food cannery, the tallest building in Winington. Technically, it was only supposed to be used by employees of the RESNIC Geological Survey Group, but the townsfolk took every chance they could to sneak up. The RESNIC folks were supposedly going to find out the mysteries of the boulder and the secrets of its levitation. They came from California in big white vans. They set up laboratories in tents all around Winington. No one knew what happened in those tents.

It took roughly 15 minutes to climb the ladder. One initial problem was people going in opposite directions. While one group was making their way down, another was going up on the ladder. This caused all sorts of chaos, with people yelling and shoving and all, so Mayor Polinsky set some protocols for using the ladder:

> *The rooftop ladder at the Winington Cat Food Cannery is private property and may only be used by the RESNIC Geological Survey Group. It is NOT for public use. If by unfortunate circumstances you find yourself in need of using the ladder, please only use it go to UP during the AM hours and only use it to go DOWN during the PM hours.*

Things became more streamlined after that, and much of the town's happenings began taking place on the boulder. The RESNIC folk didn't mind us as long as we didn't interrupt their work. Teenagers went into the caves to smoke. There was a small canyon where the young children played, jumping from one rock protrusion to the next, often getting themselves covered in scrapes and bruises. Toward the south, around a half-hour walk from the ladder, was a smooth mesa that became a popular picnic destination.

The boulder had seemingly become a part of Winington, or maybe Winington had become part of the boulder. We began hearing things like, "Just got down from the boulder so I'll be at your place in five," and "I'll meet you on the boulder near the rock pillar that looks like Elvis Presley, the one next to the Big-Ass Gorge."

The Big-Ass Gorge, aptly named because it was exactly that, quickly became a popular arts venue for its acoustic properties, as well as its relatively flat and safe terrain. The Winington Improv Comedy Troupe began performing every Wednesday night. Each time they went up the ladder, the members brought up plastic lawn chairs strapped to their backs, and in a few weeks there were enough chairs to seat an audience of a hundred. There was an art exhibit one weekend showcasing works inspired by the boulder. Famous artists came from places like Prague and Mexico City. They even had a wine and cheese reception.

When Fourth of July came around, it seemed like the entire town was up on the boulder. From the boulder we could see fireworks from all the neighboring counties. Despite the crowd, we were able secure a fairly nice area that night, just east of the Elvis Presley pillar.

"It's strange seeing fireworks from up here," you said.

"How so?" I asked.

"The lights seem so much closer. But I don't think this was the way fireworks were meant to be seen. I think whoever invented fireworks probably meant for them to be seen from the ground."

"They don't celebrate Fourth of July in Spain."

"Well, why would they? It's an American holiday."

"I'm just saying."

"Just saying what?"

"That they don't celebrate Fourth of July in Spain."

"Maybe I won't go."

"No?"

"I doubt they have a giant suspended boulder there. Winington used to be nowhere. We were all nobodies. Now Winington is finally someplace, and you, me, we're finally somebodies. Doesn't it feel great to be a somebody?"

"I guess."

* * *

Some folks, for one reason or another, did not take to the boulder. There were several incidents of people, from both Winington and out of town, shooting their firearms at the boulder, causing small chunks to come crashing down. Some were as small as pebbles and some were as big as melons. They fell on automobiles and rooftops, and sometimes people. There were many injuries and one death. Winington old-timer Douglas Wetkins, the owner of the bowling alley, was getting groceries when a piece of the boulder the size of a walnut hit him dead in the temple. The shooters all had different responses when asked why they shot at the boulder. Some thought they could scare the boulder away. Others thought they could chip away at the boulder until it was completely gone. Some of them just wanted something to shoot at. Many people wanted the shooters arrested, while others argued that there was nothing illegal about shooting a boulder. What difference did it make that the boulder was floating?

All this shooting drummed up quite a bit of conflict with a group that called itself the Order of the Boulder. They wore dark gray robes and spent most of their time chanting in circles at the town hall plaza. According to their scriptures, the boulder was actually a UFO from the Crab Nebula, roughly 6,500 light years from earth, where all life was created by a race of sentient cosmic stones. The boulder was the first of many that would arrive in an event called "The Great Recycling," when 10,000 gigantic boulder UFOs will come crashing through the Earth's surface to start the planet anew, and the souls of humankind will be merged into a soupy primordial sea, free from the burden of individual existence. The cult's sworn enemy was the RESNIC Geological Survey Group, which was apparently a front for an ancient organization dedicated to corrupting the boulder UFOs by harvesting energy from their levitation cores.

One morning when we were getting ready to go up to the boulder, we saw that the cultists had surrounded the cat food cannery. They had all sorts of improvised weaponry. Sushi knives duct-taped to broomsticks, baseballs with nails in them, hockey sticks with barbed wire at one end, meat tenderizers, and so on. They weren't letting any of the RESNIC employees go up the ladder. There was a lot of yelling and pushing and shoving. Pretty soon, RESNIC security guards showed up with rifles. I don't remember how the shooting broke out, but I do remember holding your hand tight while trying to escape all the confusion and thinking that maybe the boulder coming to Winington wasn't such a great thing after all, that it would have been better if it had appeared over New York or London or Tokyo or Cairo instead.

* * *

I remember the last time we performed together. It was the memorial concert on the boulder for the victims of the cat food cannery massacre. Twelve people were killed: eight cultists, three

RESNIC employees, and one teenager who got caught in the shooting, Margaret Hooper. She worked at the dairy on Main Street. She always gave extra ice cream toppings. She was shot through the right lung.

The concert was a small one, since only musicians with smaller instruments could come up the ladder. We played as a twelve-person chamber ensemble. We played an hour of Bach's sacred music. We all played well, but I was mostly listening to your oboe.

"If the boulder disappears or falls, I'll be leaving for Spain," you said after the concert.

"I know," I said. "Who will I practice with then?"

"Sarah the bassoon player?"

"No, her tone is awful."

"Mary Ann. She's always looking for more practice friends."

"No, I hate horn players. They're pretentious."

"Christina. I know you like Christina. She's an excellent flautist."

"I'm going to stop playing if you leave, I think."

* * *

People stopped going up to the boulder after the massacre. RESNIC was forced to leave Winington due to the shooting. And as if the boulder itself knew that its time was up, one Tuesday morning the boulder simply vanished, taking with it its secrets.

During its 80-day existence, the boulder meant many different things to a whole lot of people. For some, its existence reflected a welcome change in their routine lives. For others, it was nothing more than an interesting conversation piece. Some people thought the boulder made sense of all the chaos in the world, and others thought that the boulder, much like everything else in life, was meaningless and random. It was an opportunity for some and an obstacle for others, or simply a boulder that blocked the sun. For me, the boulder was what held you close to me, close to this town, close to the music I love so much. You never told me what the boulder meant for you. You said I wouldn't understand.

Only memories of the boulder remain. The occasional research group still shows up and takes readings of our streets with strange devices, hoping for some small trace of it, to reassure us that it had not just been our collective imaginations. Tour groups sometimes stop by to give a cursory glance at the town that had once lived under the boulder's shadow. They stop for ten or fifteen minutes before moving on to Death Valley or Las Vegas.

I wish you had disappeared that morning like the boulder did, without a trace and seemingly into thin air. I'd like to think you fell into another dimension or disappeared against your will into nothingness. But you left plenty of reminders that you are still out there, somewhere among the mountains of Madrid or the coasts of Barcelona: Your missing toothbrush that morning. The empty closet. The note you left by the nightstand.

SUSAN THORNTON HOBBY

HoCoPoLitSo
Howard County Poetry & Literature Society

presents
An Interview with **Gish Jen**

Gish Jen aims to write and rewrite America. Raised in Scarsdale, New York, by Chinese immigrant parents, Jen is both a part of and apart from her home culture, a beneficial vantage point for a writer observing the world.

Her first novel, published in 1991 about a Chinese immigrant family, begins "It's an American story." Adding to the U.S. narrative is Jen's self-proclaimed life project.

Photo © Basso Cannarsa

And in 2000, uber-American novelist John Updike, when asked to name a successor, chose her.

Born Lillian Jen and expected by family to become a doctor or lawyer, Jen started writing in high school. In her creative writing club, she took a liking to their nickname for her: Gish, for actor Lillian Gish. Adopting the name seemed a step toward her own reinvention. Though she went to Harvard as pre-med, she earned semi-dreadful grades in chemistry and emerged with an English degree.

She worked at a publishing house for a while, then compromised to practicality and her family's wishes for success, enrolling in Stanford Business School. But she took writing classes instead. After a year, she dropped out.

"I had been growing the self," Jen told an interviewer on C-Span. "I had been growing this American self that was very different from the nice Chinese girl self. I couldn't go back any more; I had to go forward."

Her parents didn't speak to her for years.

After a stint teaching English in China and a degree from the Iowa Writer's Workshop, Jen started writing short stories about immigrants (four of which were chosen for *Best American Short Stories*).

She wrote literary fiction focused on the American family—a novel about an adolescent Chinese girl converting to Judaism (*Mona in the Promised Land*), and another about a Chinese man and his white wife who adopt two Asian babies and bring over a nanny from China to grant his mother's dying wish (*The Love Wife*). She wrote nonfiction based in science to explore cultural differences between Eastern and Western approaches to selfhood and creativity (*Tiger Writing* and *The Girl at the Baggage Claim*).

Then Donald Trump was elected president, and Jen's last child went to college. The combination of those forces both frightened and freed Jen. She went rogue. She wrote dystopia. *The Resisters* was published in February 2020. Novelist Ann Patchett called it "a stone-cold masterpiece." Stephen King's blurb read "An absolute joy."

Jen's vision for the future is AutoAmerica, a branded, segregated place in which climate change has left the land flooded and devastated by storms, where angel-fair people called "the Netted" live and work on high ground, and copper-toned "Surplus" people live on boats or in swampland, are not allowed to work, and are compelled to consume. The free food distributed by "mall-trucks" likely contains sedatives. A distinctly intelligent artificial intelligence controls America, the population is microchipped and surveilled, houses are automated, and gases seep in from swamps and cripple children. But because Jen brings a wry humor to all of her work, the horrors have catchy names. Ship'EmBack is the term for the immigration policy. Genetically modified people are HomoUpgraded. The internet has blended with artificial intelligence to become Aunt Nettie. And politicians are DelectableElectables.

Jen populates this world with a family: Grant, a former English professor of Caribbean descent; Eleanor, an Asian former immigration lawyer who now fights for the rights of the children harmed by swamp Emanations; and their Blasian daughter Gwen, a savant at baseball pitching who started by hurling stuffed animals from her crib. Sports, specifically the upstart underground baseball team that the family founds, becomes a form of resistance, influenced, Jen has said, by the NFL's Colin Kaepernick taking a knee during the anthem.

"The magic of Gish Jen's latest novel is that, amid a dark and cautionary tale, there's a story also filled with electricity and humor—and baseball," the *Washington Post* review reads. So, yes, there's trouble in this dark dystopia, but *The Resisters* is also about hope. Jen sometimes writes about the Chinese maxim *chi ku*, which means to eat bitterness.

"In a general kind of way, that's assumed to be part of life by the Chinese, that you eat bitterness," Jen told me. "It doesn't have as negative a connotation as it does here, because it's associated with endurance. Here, we assume that life is going to be easy and we're trying to be happy. But they assume that life is going to be really hard, and the triumph comes not with being happy, the triumph comes with surviving."

Jen has survived, and thrived, in the publishing world. The 1980s weren't chockablock with Chinese American novelists—Maxine Hong Kingston and Amy Tan blazed a trail, but Jen saw her spot on the path. Before *The Resisters*, Jen published five novels, two works of nonfiction, and a collection of short stories, and her work has appeared in *The New Yorker* and *The Atlantic Monthly*, as well as other periodicals and anthologies.

All good writing is subversive, Jen claims, and she's very fond of the quote from Thomas Hardy, "Literature is the written expression of revolt against accepted things."

I interviewed Jen on an October evening in 2020, with classical piano music playing in her home.

Little Patuxent Review: At one point you were pre-med, and then you went to Stanford Business School. But you always loved literature. When did you decide to become a writer, and how did that go over with your family?

Gish Jen: It did not go over at all well. I was confused for some time. I did work in publishing for a while. I realized I was half doing what I wanted, halfway into the world I wanted to be in, and halfway into the other world that seemed more practical. I decided if I couldn't decide which direction to go, I should just try the more practical route first. So I applied to business school, which was the one thing I had never had any interest in. I don't know what possessed me, to be honest. I guess because I had already eliminated medical school and law school.

Weirdly enough, I got into both Harvard and Stanford. But I went to Stanford because I knew they had a good writing program. As soon as I got there, I realized I was in the wrong place. The very first day I was at business school, I had no idea what they're talking about, and what's more, I really couldn't care less. I spent my whole first year of business school reading novels and taking writing classes. I read 100 novels. The second year rolled around, and the first day of class I overslept. The second day of class I overslept. I overslept the third day. By the end of the first week, I realized I was never going to be able to get myself to go to class.

So I dropped out. My parents were Chinese immigrants, and of course this was way before anybody thought an Asian American could be a novelist, right? They were totally, totally, totally upset, stopped speaking to me for years. It was pretty terrible. But we all survived. It seems like a long time ago now. Now that I'm a parent, I understand a little bit better where they were coming from, what financial security actually means. I understand how insecure a writer's life is.

LPR: For a year, you taught English in a Chinese coal-mining city. How was that experience?

GJ: It was formative. It was quite early, it was 1981. So China would only have been open for a little while. I was the only foreigner in the whole half of the city where I was, a huge city, Jinan, in Shandong [province]. It was extremely exciting for me, in part because that was when my real understanding of cultural difference came. I grew up with cultural difference, but I had a much deeper understanding after having lived in China. Obviously, because my parents were Chinese immigrants, I knew a lot. But I knew a lot more after I had lived in their home culture for a while. There are so many things I could see around me that were just like my parents, the way people thought. Of course, that interest has gone on to inform my entire career.

LPR: Could you talk about your immigrant or second-generation immigrant stories? You've written many of them, "Mr. Crime and Punishment and War and Peace" and other short stories, *Typical American*, the Wong family in *The Love Wife* and *Mona*?

GJ: There was a way in which I wanted to claim American literature for people like me. It's not just "I know this little piece of land, I'll write about that." It was definitely a claiming of literature and a claiming of America for groups that had not gotten any attention whatsoever really. . . . I've always seen myself not as only writing about the immigrant experience, but really rewriting America, about the American experiment.

LPR: Mama Wong in *The Love Wife* has many maxims, and Grant remembers many of his mother's sayings in *The Resisters*: "a secret is a shame or a treasure." Are those sayings you remember or that you invented? And why are they there?

GJ: I invented them, I made that up. I guess because, don't we all hear things that other people have said that we remember? That's part of the way we are in the world. It's in *World and Town* [her 2010 novel]. It's not just mothers, it's things their husbands said, their wives said. It's one of the ways we hold onto our past. My husband will say, "You know what your mother always says: 'Everything in moderation.'" It's one of the ways that she still lives with us....

LPR: In *Tiger Writing*, could you explain your line, "How much more the novel knows than the writer who wrote it"?

GJ: There are all these things that you don't realize you know. And then when you write it, you realize, oh, I guess I do know that. Your writing is smarter than you are. There are all these things you've picked up, that you forget you've picked up, you don't remember anybody telling you, like a lot of these Chinese idioms. If you asked me, "Could you name four Chinese idioms?" I would say, "No, I can't think of any." But my character just spouted them out. Where did that come from? It's also about the nature of the world. A lot of things will happen, in your novel, that maybe you haven't lived yourself, you don't know directly, but you know that's how it happened.

LPR: How does *The Resisters* flow from your stories of immigration and your nonfiction about cultural differences?

GJ: I have imagined myself writing about the American project the whole way. So if you think about it that way, it's a very natural follow-on. I'm still writing about America. I've written about outsiderness all the way as well. Outsiderness as a source of not just of alienation but power. There's a way in which this little family [in *The Resisters*], which is so isolated—in a way it's just like my family; we were kind of isolated. In a way, it was a bad thing, but also a good thing.... In a funny kind of way, because we're not so tied into society, we have enough leeway to set our own agenda. Growing up, we didn't belong to any clubs; you would think, that's terrible, but when I got to college, it was clear to me a lot of the ways that other women had been socialized, I wasn't socialized like that. I didn't have all these ideas that you had to wear good clothes.

I understood that, in a funny kind of way, that being such an outsider is sort of a privilege. It's sort of liberating; you can see that in *The Resisters*. There's a weird way that they can say what they want, and pursue things that they want to do, partly because they're so isolated.... They can pursue these activities in these marooned places that they would never be able to pursue in spaces that were more regulated. There, too, there's a way in which the spaces become islands of innovation.... In that way, it's a little bit like, these people are still like me, immigrants, or outsiders of some kind. Gwen's experiences at Net U [the college for the Netted society] are first-gen experiences right down the line. It's not like I sat down and said, "What did I feel like being first-gen at college?" But I knew how she would feel—this is "the writing knows more than the writer."

LPR: The family at the heart of *The Resisters* has made a cozy kind of life, with their garden and their knitting and their worm composting. It's a pioneer sensibility they have.

GJ: It's sort of uncomfortable. No one would choose to live where they're living. But they've made it their own. They're inventive people. As you gather, Eleanor is Surplus almost voluntarily. She has the option to leave, but she doesn't leave as a matter of principle. She is working within the system, but there's a way in which she just cannot participate in the social order as it is constructed, in that kind of oppression. I live in northern Vermont, and a lot of people here have basically dropped out. It's not that they couldn't have a job at fill-in-the-blank. They just chose not to participate in that, within the capitalist system as they understood it. So they are resisters.

LPR: There are so many issues in *The Resisters*—climate change, income inequality, racism, internet takeover, privacy invasion, failure of democracy, overconsumption—these are all the things I wake up at 3 o'clock in the morning and worry about. Your book is dystopian fiction, yes, but you're taking today's problems just a little bit further.

GJ: What happened was that I was sitting down—my daughter had just started college, so I was an empty-nester—in the first moments, of oh my gosh, complete control over my day for the first time in 30 years. I can just write whatever I want. That's also part of the reason I went and did this crazy thing, because I just sat through freshman orientation, and I heard every five minutes, "Explore, have fun." So I come home, and I think I should explore and have fun. That was partly why the book came out so wild. . . .

Because I have a daughter going to college, and I'm thinking about the future, as you will when you have a freshman in college, I'm thinking about the world that she will be entering, and it's scary. This whole world is something to be quite concerned about. Even though she's left the house and I don't have to write anything having to do with parental responsibility, nonetheless apparently I can't really escape my own sense of parental responsibility. I go on to write a book that really is about where we could be basically if you, daughter, don't take your studies seriously. You've got to do something. You can almost look at it as a laundry list of things that she could think about doing with her studies. Here are some of the problems of the world, any one of which is worthy of your attention. . . .

You can also see the great hope that I have in the future. You can see the many forms of resistance that are possible. You can see all the problems, but you can also see so many ways that you can resist. Also the hope, or the faith really, that the young will resist. I do think that they're up to the job. I guess I have to hope that. I think it's going to take everything they have, and they're going to have to work together. We need them to step up to the plate and hit that ball out of the park.

LPR: The product names in *The Resisters* are hilarious: Disarm'Em, SpritzGram, HomoUpgrade, BSDetect, Gonad Wrap, DelectableElectables. How did you come up with those?

GJ: I had a lot of fun. I was just fooling around. You can see from *Mona*, I've always liked to fool around with language, it's so reflexive, it's just the way I am. . . . Part of it may be that words are funny to me partly because my parents spoke another language—there's just a little alienation between me and the language. I can kind of see the words. You should only be aware of their meaning, but I'm aware of the words themselves. I think that is a result of having bilingual parents.

LPR: We have to talk about baseball. I love Grant's idea of baseball being like an agrarian society. There's something both communal and independent in baseball, unlike a lot of other sports. Is that why you chose this sport, or are you just a big baseball person?

GJ: Baseball is the American sport, right? I'm writing about America, and if you can write America and you use a sport, baseball is America. Because it's surfing the balance between urban and agrarian. There's a way in which it's harking back to our farmer days—we all stare at this big green thing. Right in the middle of a city, you have this field of dreams. The whole idea that it's this ideal balance between the team and the individual. The whole idea that you have these rules, with the idea that these agreed-upon rules will help us actualize ourselves. To people from foreign countries, this is a very weird idea. . . . Baseball harkens back to our farming days in that it goes until the job is done; there's no clock. Unlike other sports, which are on more of an industrial mold. . . . [Baseball] is like when you bring in the harvest; you work until it's done, that's how long you're out there. . . .

I also had an emotional understanding of what baseball meant. This is the outsider thing. One of the first ways my parents became American was going to a baseball game. Every immigrant will tell you this: "We went to a baseball game and we had a hot dog; we learned the words to 'Take Me Out to the Ball Game.'" In my family's case, my mother became this avid, avid baseball fan. That was America for her. She did die of COVID a couple months ago. But we buried her with a Yankees cap. What baseball meant to her, I understood not only intellectually what baseball was, but I understood emotionally, when we come to America, you want to know what it means to be an American, it's all tied to baseball. . . .

LPR: You've included many quotations about democracy in *The Resisters*—the epigraph from Lincoln, "Let us have faith that might makes right," the Gettysburg address, Patrick Henry, the Letter from a Birmingham Jail. Why remind us so much about democracy?

GJ: I will say that I did sit down to write this book in September of 2017, and I think it was already apparent that we had a large problem on our hands. There's a way in which you're always writing for the ages, but at the time I sat down, I just felt new urgency. I had been writing about the American project since the beginning, but there was a new urgency around democracy, and it's continued until this moment. I don't think it's over with this election, I'm sorry to say.

LPR: Eleanor [the mother in *The Resisters*] is always fighting. Her catchphrase is "And now where were we, we have work to do." You dedicate the book to "all the Eleanors I know." Is there a particular kind of woman you modeled Eleanor after?

GJ: Eleanor is an admirable person. I definitely know people for whom justice is the first thing they think of in the morning and the last thing they thing about at night. It's a tremendous privilege to know people like that.

LPR: Was *The Resisters* meant to be a warning? Or a call to action? Or just a great story?

GJ: All of the above. It's a cautionary tale. But they're working together in quite a laudable way. We all wish they didn't have so much to resist. So it is a call to action to people of today to please do something before the world looks like this. But at the same time, it is a lot of fun. It's funny, and I think there's a lot in the family dynamic that people can relate to, regardless of whether the planet has been flooded or not.

Visitation

He's on the front step when I open the door to get the morning papers. Sun-bleached, shoulder-length hair; deep-set eyes the blue of motel swimming pools. He's wearing cutoff jeans and a faded Sticky Fingers t-shirt. He looks amazing, for sixty-three.

"Charlie?" I clutch the neck of my robe. I must be dreaming. "I thought you were—"

"Dead?" A grin unfolds. He always enjoyed proving me wrong. "Who told you that, Leda?"

"My mother. I was living in Buenos Aires at the time, which is why I didn't go to the funeral. But I sent your parents flowers and a card."

"Well, your mom's never liked me."

It's been a cold, wet fall in Maryland. Charlie's barefoot and shivering, lips purple like they used to be after a dawn session in the surf. He'd rest his arms on my windowsill, whistling low until I woke up. The house I grew up in was Spanish-style, with wrought iron bars on the windows. "Señorita," he'd whisper. "Let me in." I'd tiptoe out to the hallway, past the frowning ancestor portraits, and slowly slide open the patio door. I wouldn't let him touch me until he'd been under the covers a while—his hands were like ice, from the ocean.

Later, he'd crouch in my closet among the shoes, tennis racket, and field hockey stick while I put on my school uniform, gulped orange juice. "You're so flushed," my mother would say. "You shouldn't take such long showers. Your father will have a fit about the water bill." He'd have left for work already, before the Pasadena Freeway became a nightmare.

My mother drove my younger sister and me to school, a round trip long enough for Charlie to emerge from his hiding place, calmly eat a bowl of Cheerios, stack his dish with the others in the sink. The milk, cereal, and bananas were never missed.

* * *

"Come in before you freeze," I say now, and Charlie tracks wet leaves onto the carpet.

"Don't want to wake your folks," he whispers.

"*My folks?*" Who are pushing ninety in a retirement home in Santa Barbara.

Just then Joe clatters down the stairs in his wingtips. He's interviewing the vice president today, has on a coat and tie, his beard neatly trimmed. Absurdly, I feel proud of his dapper appearance.

"Joe, honey—this is Charlie."

"Your high school boyfriend Charlie?"

"Yes, he's just arrived, from—"

"California," Charlie says.

Joe's unflappability is what makes him such a good reporter. He smiles. "I've heard a lot about you."

"If I were polite, I'd say the same," Charlie says.

"How about breakfast?" Joe says. "I understand you like Cheerios."

* * *

Breakfast is Joe's specialty, but Charlie refuses his offer of a cinnamon-laced cappuccino. "Tried coffee once, hated it," he says.

"I remember—at the House of Pie on Colorado Boulevard," I say, joining them at the table. I've been sick and should be in bed, but Charlie's appearance is a miracle. "It was before the trig final. You said it gave you the shakes."

"Aced the class, though."

"Ha, so did I," Joe says. "What'd you get on the math SAT?"

"Seven-ninety."

"My man. Seven-eighty-six." They high-five. "*My* parents paid off nobody," brags my husband, who forked over plenty for our boys to be tutored. "Do you like your eggs over easy?"

"Oh, yeah."

"Bacon?"

"Hell, yeah," Charlie says. "Don't want to make you late, though." See, he can be polite when he feels like it.

But Joe's delighted—I'm a tea-and-toast breakfaster, and since the boys left home his short-order chops have gone unappreciated. He ties one dish towel around his neck, tucks another into his belt.

While he's at the stove, I study Charlie, who's perusing the headlines. He was an old-looking eighteen, and I can't really tell if he's changed. Though the same is true when I examine my own face in the mirror—only in photos can I perceive the passage of time.

Joe twists the dishtowels around his hands to carry plates to the table. "Careful, they're hot," he says, in a professional tone. He fry-cooked his way through college.

Charlie bends low over his food, shoveling, gripping the

silverware like handlebars. His table manners were one of the many things my mother held against him. "This is primo," he says.

"Leda never lets me eat like this anymore," Joe exults with his mouth full.

"Do you take anything for high blood pressure or cholesterol?" I ask Charlie.

"Why would I?" he asks, wiping his mouth with the back of his wrist.

* * *

Charlie's heart, my mother told me on the phone thirty years ago, was in perfect condition after the accident. It went to somebody waiting for a transplant, saved a life. "So in the end," she said, "he did something unselfish."

I burst into tears and hung up on her.

It's true she never liked him; on the other hand, why would she invent his death? I wasn't still pining for him—I was newly married, with a journalism career in another hemisphere.

Charlie's parents never answered my condolence note, though I didn't expect them to. But what if there'd been a mistake? They must have been baffled, wondering if I'd lost my mind down there in South America.

* * *

Joe glances at his Fitbit, jumps up. "Shit, *now* I'm late."

"I follow him to the front door. "Joe, I'm sorry about this," I murmur. "I had no idea Charlie was coming. I had no idea he was *alive*."

"Remember what they taught us in J-school—if your mom says she loves you, check it out."

"Never had to chase that one down," I say, smiling. "Anyway, it's nice you're getting along."

Joe shrugs. "We do have something in common. Can you believe how close our math scores were?"

* * *

It was 1975 when Charlie Grafton showed up at the Chesterfield School in Pasadena in similar unannounced fashion.

Strode into the headmaster's office, said he'd heard the place offered the best education around and could he go. He didn't have money to pay though.

The school secretary was taken aback. Charlie was tall and gaunt. Bare feet and raggedy clothes were stylish then, but not when applying to a fancy private day school.

"You'd have to take a test," she began.

"I'll take it right now."

She looked alarmed—Charlie told me later—like she thought he might pull a knife or something.

The headmaster, Mr. Brown, came out and suggested that this unusual young man take a walk with him. Charlie was arrogant, sure, but he had a sweet, disarming curiosity. He asked and repeated the name of each flowering tree in the school courtyard: jacaranda, oleander, camellia, bottlebrush. He'd never seen such flora—and fauna, he added, pointing to a flock of parrots Mr. Brown informed him were the descendants of escaped pets. Charlie then told Mr. Brown that the moment he first dipped his feet into the Pacific Ocean, a week earlier, was the happiest of his life.

He scored higher than anyone ever had on the entrance test. And it turned out there was a scholarship available—the school's first and only black student had recently transferred to a boarding school back East.

"All over" was where Charlie usually said he was from. He had a brother in jail in Ohio. His father worked as a repo man, taking away appliances people had missed payments on, though he wasn't scary-looking or even very big. His mother was enormous and pale, unlike all the suntanned, tennis-dressed mothers I knew, who smoked to stay thin. Mrs. Grafton and I discovered we followed the same soap opera and spent hours merrily deploring the wickedness of Erica Kane.

Her own health problems she didn't care to discuss; enthroned on a gold plush recliner, she'd occasionally pause the conversation to wheeze and fan herself with the book of crossword puzzles propped against her bosom. The only other books in the house were from the library, in Charlie's room. He always got himself a card first thing, whenever they arrived someplace new.

Much later, he confessed that he asked me out after realizing I was the best student in English class—he figured reading would give us something to talk about.

* * *

Back in the kitchen, Charlie's got the Post open to the funnies. "*Doonesbury*'s great today," he says. "Did you see it?"

I sit down at the table, pour a stewed second cup of tea. "Charlie, how exactly did you get here?"

He looks up. He's got on the gold-rimmed aviators he wore only in class. "In the Veedub."

"It's still running?"

"I do the repairs myself."

A head-on collision on the Pacific Coast Highway—that was what my mother said. A foggy early morning, someone drifting sleepy or drunk across the median. This had happened once when I was with him. If we hadn't swerved, the Volkswagen would have crumpled like tinfoil.

"Your car's not out front," I say.

"Habit,' Charlie says, with a sly smile. When we were teenagers, he'd park a few blocks away so my father wouldn't twig the sunrise rendezvous with his supposedly sleeping daughter.

I feel myself blushing. "So, what have you been up to, since graduation?"

His expression clouds. "Since *your* graduation, you mean?"

Chesterfield wouldn't give him a diploma. He had the grades, but once he discovered surfing, he basically quit going to school. He was told he could march with the class and receive a blank folder.

"Bullshit," he said to Mr. Brown. "I want a diploma." He'd be the first in his family to get one. But on this point—unlike many others, where concessions were made because he really was a brilliant student—the headmaster held firm.

"You shouldn't have sworn at him," I'd said. We were packing his car for a road trip after the ceremony. I'd changed to shorts and a t-shirt under my graduation gown, the white dress I was supposed to be wearing folded into my book bag.

"*Bullshit* isn't swearing."

"You can't say it on TV." This kind of semantic argument we could pursue at length, even not stoned. "Besides, you didn't follow the rules," I said.

"Damn straight. I'll wait for you on the Arroyo Bridge."

The plan was that I'd sneak away from the reception and we'd head up Highway One, camping and surfing along the way. Not many girls surfed in those days, and Charlie promised to teach me. We had army surplus sleeping bags and a kerosene stove. I'd said I'd teach Charlie to cook, though I didn't know how to do that, either. A milk crate of books we'd picked out at a used book store: *Under the Volcano, The Eustace Diamonds, Memento Mori, The End of the Affair, Daniel Deronda, Casanova's Chinese Restaurant, The Moviegoer*.

My little sister, Penny, bored during the ceremony, began fiddling with my backpack and pulled out the white dress. I was onstage at the time, giving a speech, so couldn't concoct an explanation before my parents guessed the truth. When I'd announced I was going on this trip with Charlie, they'd said no, I wasn't. I'm eighteen, I'd said. An unassailable position, I believed.

But they had another, presented through gritted-teeth smiles as we posed for photos: if I went on this trip, they would not pay for college. Not one dime. I'd be on my own, forever.

* * *

"So you see," I say now, "I had no choice." I'd seen Charlie's car on the Arroyo Bridge, as my family's Country Squire rounded the corner. He was sitting on the hood with his head lowered, arms resting on his knees. What I never knew was whether he'd seen our car and was heartbroken, or was reading something open on his lap.

Charlie shakes his head. "They were bluffing."

"I didn't think so at the time."

"So you went anyway."

"All the way to Oregon. It was fucking cold, but gorgeous."

"So I heard."

That fall, from my freshman dorm, I'd called Charlie's house. "He's still up north," his mother said. "He says it's pretty country."

"Oh, that's wonderful," I burbled.

"You hurt him." I waited for her to say something more, but after saying *Mrs. Grafton, Mrs. Grafton* a few times and hearing nothing but her soft, wheezy breathing, I hung up.

* * *

"I met a girl up near Medford," Charlie says.

I look down at my hands—those new, big freckles. Liver spots, my grandmother called hers. "I'm glad."

He laughs. "Liar." He reaches across the table, takes my wrist between two fingers as if reading my pulse. "You're pretty cute in that old-lady bathrobe, Leda."

I giggle slightly and pull away. "We should maintain distance, Charlie."

"I'd say we've done that. What's it—forty-five years now?"

"I mean I've had the virus. Joe and I both did. We tested negative, but I'm having recurring symptoms."

Charlie shakes his head, as if this is more of my bullshit. "You probably just need some fresh air. We could drive to the beach."

"Now? It's three hours to the Eastern Shore."

"Suit yourself." He gets up and goes to the bookshelf, runs a finger along the spines, then pulls out *Infinite Jest*.

"That's my older son's favorite," I say.

He hefts it. "Seems like Dave Wallace could've used an editor."

"David Foster Wallace," I say.

"Excuse *me*, Miss Fancypants." But he sits down with the book in the armchair by the window.

"I'm sorry," I say.

He looks up, holds my gaze. "I'm listening, Leda."

"It was nice of you to come all this way, but going to the beach isn't practical. Why don't we walk around the neighborhood, instead? I'll take a shower, get dressed. You'll have to wear a mask, but we have extra."

"I'm that ugly, huh?"

Now it's my turn to laugh. "Charlie, there's a worldwide pandemic on, in case you haven't heard."

"Nope." He turns back to the novel. "This is good, actually. Take your time."

Upstairs in the bedroom, I Google Charlie and there's nothing, not even an obit.

It's early in California, but I telephone my sister and ask her if she remembers him. There are seven years between us, so we had separate childhoods, but with common elements we've spent our adult lives exhuming, like a two-person crime lab.

"Vaguely," Penny says sleepily. "Long blond hair? Was he the guy who taught me to ride a unicycle?"

"I forgot about the unicycle," I say. "Yup, that was Charlie." I tell her about graduation, the white dress in the backpack, the aborted road trip.

"Oh, my god, I have no memory of that," Penny says. "I ruined your life, and I don't even remember."

"You didn't ruin my life," I say.
"He wasn't your one great love?"
"No, that's been Joe, definitely."
"Phew, then," Penny says.
"I just wish I'd defied Mom and Dad. If I'd gone on the trip, I could have encouraged him to get a GED, go to junior college."
"Wait—was he the one who died in that car crash?"
"Uh-huh. Except—" Downstairs I hear footsteps, then the toilet flush in the powder room. "Did you read about the accident in the paper?"
"No, I was at college. Mom told me." After a pause, she asks, "How are you feeling today, love?"
"Why do you ask?"
"I don't know, you sound a little feverish."

* * *

There's no point in calling my mother to see what she recalls. She and my father have forgotten everything. Well—they still know my name. They thank me profusely for calling, ask when I'm coming to visit. *When all this is over*, I tell them.

* * *

"Just tell them you're going," Charlie said, looking up from the Triple A map he was marking with a yellow highlighter. We were upstairs in his room. We could do whatever we wanted in there—his mom wasn't able to climb stairs. "What are your folks going to do, beat you?"
I froze. "Of course not," I said. *Now it's just a joke: Do I need to get the belt, my father might say, smiling at the dinner table, as if it never happened for real.*

* * *

I get into the shower. As the hot water pours over my face I open my eyes for a moment and see the pink-and-white tiles of my girlhood bathroom. I squeeze them shut.
While I'm getting dressed, time folds back again. I'm in in my old California bedroom, with its sprigged poppy wallpaper. Hooked over the closet door is my graduation dress in its dressmaker bag.

Hands shaking, I open the door. Nobody's there.

I feel dizzy, so I lie on the bed for a minute and close my eyes. When I open them, I'm back in Joe's and my room, with its scuffed walls covered by framed snapshots that are always going crooked, the sliding piles of magazines. The light is dim. I check my phone; it's after five p.m.

Even before I go downstairs, I know Charlie won't be there anymore. But in the powder room, the seat's left up, something my husband never does. I put it down. I'm vacuuming the leaves from the carpet when Joe walks in.

"You shouldn't be doing that," he says. "You seemed to have a temperature this morning, so I tried not to wake you."

"I'm better now. But I didn't make anything for dinner."

"I'll fix us some eggs." He opens the fridge. "Except we're out. I could've sworn—well, how about grilled cheese?"

"Perfect," I say, and sit down at the table still greasy from breakfast. That's when I notice *Infinite Jest* is gone—there's a missing-tooth gap on the shelf. When Charlie liked a book, he'd read it all the way through without stopping, no matter what else we had planned. *Ti-i-ime is on my side*, he'd sing, if I complained.

RACHELE SALVINI

Stellar

My grandparents met at a theater in Livorno in the fifties. My grandpa laughed so hard that he broke his seat and fell over the girl sitting in the row behind him: my grandma.

A story from a Hollywood romantic comedy.

In the musicals of the Golden Age, the characters stopped the clocks and started dancing and singing in a parallel universe. Dance was sexual attraction, emotional and physical rapture. The numbers were short voyages in galaxies of dreams.

Valerio and I went to the movies in London to see *La La Land* a few months before I moved to America. I had already booked the flight: our breakup date was printed on the ticket. Valerio visited me in London for the last time.

For as long as I could remember, my grandparents didn't like each other. Maybe my grandpa's seat snapping on my grandma's knees was a sign for a doomed relationship, a spoiler for how things would go. My grandma told me stories of their young love: they drove their Vespa at the Livorno seaside, their hair all dry from the salt and the libeccio. They clambered up the dirt roads in Tuscany among the cypress trees that pierced the starred sky. My grandpa worked and studied hard to become a surgeon; my grandma wanted to start a family. At the time, there was nothing more important.

In the famous scene of the skating rink in Central Park in *Shall We Dance*, Fred Astaire and Ginger Rogers sit on a bench and declare that they can never possibly fall for each other. They have different accents that bleed with class implications, and therefore they have nothing in common. Still, when they get up and start dancing on their roller-skates, their chemistry is obvious through the virtuoso dance moves of the number. They dance and sing like magic is happening under everyone's eyes, and the audience demands a happy ending.

A few months after I moved to America, Valerio told me that his life had lost its colors. When we were together, we would roll into our favorite nightclub in Livorno like John Travolta and Olivia Newton-John in *Grease*. In the school ball scene, they make their way through the crowd dancing like no one is watching—and literally everyone is.

During my first months in the United States, I forgot about all the fights we had when I worked and studied in London and was completely alone, while Valerio was at home in Livorno, partying with our friends constantly. I forgot the miscommunication and the resentment; I forgot my jealousy and his laziness; I erased our complete inability to face the future together. But these weren't the colors I wanted to remember: I tried to hold on to our dances, still perfectly synchronized in my memories.

One day, my grandma had to sew a pocket back on my grandpa's tweed coat because a patient had tried to shove money in his pocket, and my grandpa had yanked his coat away. He would give free physicals to people he liked, which was basically everyone.

He made a lot of money as a surgeon, but he was very generous. He loved his job, our city, and our people. My grandma, instead, had one goal in life: family had to stay united. She wanted to keep her husband and her children close.

How disappointing it must have been to discover that even family is hard to keep.

La La Land is full of references to the great musicals from the Golden Age. In my favorite number, "A Lovely Night," Ryan Gosling starts singing while swinging around a lamppost, like Gene Kelly in *Singin' in the Rain*. He and Emma Stone tap-dance on a bench in Griffith Park, Los Angeles, just like Fred Astaire and Ginger Rogers on their bench in Central Park in *Shall We Dance*. The protagonists of *La La Land* don't really hit it off, but throughout the movie they keep bumping into each other in the city as if driven by destiny, as if their love is—big rom-com cliché coming—*written in the stars*.

As inevitable as it is, the mutual antipathy turns into attraction, then love. *What a shame we're the ones that are experiencing this beautiful view*, Ryan Gosling's character says. Like Fred Astaire, he says that romance could never happen. She's absolutely not his type; there's no spark in sight. Emma Stone's character feels exactly the same. They keep insulting and annoying each other with moves that keep referring to screwball comedy: he kicks some dust on her feet, licks his finger, and tries to touch her face. But they also start dancing, and sparks finally arrive. Eventually, the night really does turn lovely. The audience still expects the happy ending.

When I go back to Livorno after a year in America and I see Valerio holding hands with a blonde girl, I'm smoking one of my thin cigarettes and he's drinking his usual gin and tonic. We lock eyes and I remember *La La Land*'s ending: the protagonists decide to split up and follow their dreams. Emma Stone's character becomes an actress and gets married to someone else; Ryan Gosling's ends up being a successful musician and entrepreneur. When they see each other again, years after their breakup, they look at each other from afar and eventually smile. As their love theme starts playing, we're catapulted into the last number: a fantasy of how their lives could have been, if they had decided to stay together. They dance through the corridors of an irretrievable past and an impossible future. The dances are the colors that stayed. The dream of their life together is one last, spectacular number.

My mom was in the middle of a flip on the living room rug when she saw a letter being pushed under the doorsill of my grandparents' house. She grabbed it and brought it to my grandma, who was cleaning turnip tops in the kitchen sink. She opened the letter, hands still wet, and started reading in silence. My mom was a little girl, but she understood. She had the same feeling whenever women called and asked for her father on the phone. She knew something wasn't quite right.

I can't remember if my mom ever read the letter; I'm not sure she could actually read at the time. She said that my grandma threw the letter in the trash and told her to go back to play. But then, later, my mom went to my grandparents' room to play grownup and put on my grandma's fur coats and high heels. As she looked for her mother's pearl necklace in the drawer of the vanity, she found the letter, still wet, smelling like turnip tops.

My grandma kicked my grandpa out more than once, but she always took him back: family had to stay united. When he finally retired, he got sick almost immediately and was diagnosed with Parkinson's and Alzheimer's. My grandma had to take care of the man who cheated on her and humiliated her: a final effort to maintain a façade of unity.

We don't see any of this in Hollywood comedies. Even in *La La Land*, when the protagonists break up we have a hint of a happy ending: a smile from afar and an attempt to tell a narrative of lives and choices that makes sense. Valerio squeezing the hand of a blonde girl and me, happy with my career in America. It was the right call.

As Valerio and I left the London theater after watching *La La Land*, I grabbed a promotional flyer of the movie.

"The feel-good movie of the year?" Valerio read. His eyelashes were sticky and wet from all the crying. "That movie fucking killed me."

A thin, insistent rain wet my fingers as I reached for the umbrella in my purse. The city was soaked with a thick fog, pierced by the lights of the theater. Cabs and red double-decker buses ran around us.

"Your face will ache from smiling," I read in the review by *The Sun*.

"It's hard to imagine any 2017 movie that will leave you on a higher high," Valerio read.

I opened the umbrella and shoved the flyer in my purse. At the time I was too upset by the movie's ending to realize that we could have danced like Gene Kelly, singing in the rain.

My grandfather died, but my grandma kept the family united: everyone except for me. She hasn't forgiven me yet for leaving Livorno and moving to America. In my apartment in small-town Oklahoma, I still have the old *La La Land* flyer from that London theater: it's all creased, hanging above my bed, with Ryan Gosling and Emma Stone standing between the bench and the lamp post in Griffith Park. The sky above is dotted with five-star rows from all the positive reviews. *The Guardian*'s is still my favorite: "a sun-drenched masterpiece."

Holding Sunlight

An overabundance of morning
glides slantwise
through lattice panes in the balcony door,
spreads across the carpet like a path
pebbled with shadow, embraces
my five-month-old daughter, warm and squinting,
her arms outstretched,
her pudgy fingers wrapped in gold,
scraping the matted pile, trying
again and again to hold bricks of light
in her unpracticed hands. This is how I want to live—ever
reaching, never
grasping, something weightless
grasping me.

ELYSE THOMAS

Vignette of a Puerto Rican Summer

June surges in my lungs like a salsa.
    Travels across my diaphragm

as I gather myself in a tempo.
    Swivels my hips into the pelvic

canyons of another. Forgets I am here
    for a split second while I wash away

against the coast of San Juan.
    I want to carry this full-bellied

summer with me long enough to taste
    it into winter. To not forget this wind

of Spanish that sags at the outline
    of my skin in envelopes of spiced besos.

Tell me when I'll know to stop
    riding the backs of coquí frogs

into the heatstroke of a bruised,
    velvet sky. My body, dotted

in the freckled stars
    of my gazing ancestors,

yearns to be forgotten here.
    How do I even begin to fill

this gapped ribcage
    with a beached love

for a country that breathes
    through me for only one season?

When will I know
    this has been enough?

ABDU MONGO ALI

A Conversation with Featured Artist s.e.a.

Existing in a world where profit is valued over life, one who dreams to disrupt any of the roots sprouted by consciousness of this violent ideology must queer their lens. Queering our lens is a necessary action that can be done in infinite ways. Whether it's through the freedom dreaming theories of the black queer feminist Audre Lorde or the altering image building of filmmaker Tourmaline, we need to queer our lens culturally, politically, and creatively so we can imagine different possibilities of experiencing this earth that fosters space for all life to be able to coexist holistically.

    Many provocateurs choose to wield their social altering sorcery through political activism or education or through their art. Brooklyn-based photographer Suzanne E. Abramson has been queering the lens of women's bodies of color, black joy, and what it means to be in community for more than 20 years. Born in St. Croix, s.e.a. has let her passion for photography take her from her hometown to Miami, and finally to New York City. Through documenting queer night life to photographing portraits, s.e.a. beacons the glee of queer intimacy without negotiating with spectators, thus creating visual remote paradises that emanate empowerment.

—Abdu Mongo Ali

Abdu Mongo Ali: I want to know more about you as a person. You were born and raised in St. Croix.

s.e.a.: My first 17, 18 years. My dad was born and raised there. His side of the family is under our matriarch, who passed early this year, and she was a great, scary, ball-buster of a woman. And my mom was a white lady who came down to teach young kids on the island with a whole bunch of other teachers from Boston, some program. And these ladies just fell in love with black men and married them and stayed down there and had a whole bunch of little brown babies.

And it was a great childhood. I talk to my sister about this all the time and a lot of other biracial friends of mine. We were raised in this wonderful island community that had every culture, every nationality, every race—we had people from all over the world.

I was a little tomboy; I never wanted to wear a dress. My parents never had a problem with that. They never had a problem with me not dating boys. We didn't talk about that stuff, but they never discouraged me from being who I was, and I think that that was invaluable. By the time I was 10, I knew that I was gay and had the understanding that everybody knew who my family was. It's a really tiny island. It's like 50,000, 60,000 people, and I thought, "Okay, well, I just got to be gay undercover," which means not doing anything with anybody or telling anybody anything, just pretending that I'm straight so I can get off of this island, which I did.

And the first time I went home after college, I was hanging out with a bunch of my friends, and I told them, "I got to be really honest with you, I think I'm gay." They were like, "Oh, really cool, that's awesome. We knew you were, and we're going to a gay party tonight actually...." And I was just shocked. My island is very welcoming, very friendly.

AMA: So in your household, you were basically allowed to be you.

s.e.a.: Absolutely.

AMA: I always talk about the importance of raising carefree black and brown children and how radical that is, how revolutionary that is to allow your black and brown babies to have autonomy, to have a childhood where they can fully be themselves, and you not look at them as subordinate or people you got to correct or get straight. Allowing them to be free in their bodies and in their spirit.

s.e.a.: I'm getting chills right now because that's how I grew up. Our school was an old hotel that was on the water. Our nature science class—we'd open up the back door and go out to the beach. Carefree. Saturday morning, I'd get up, have my breakfast, watch my Saturday morning cartoon, and then I would be out the door playing with my little friend in the neighborhood in the bush until it got dark. My mother had no idea what we were doing but knew that there was enough community around that people would see what we were doing, would keep us out of trouble.

AMA: How powerful it is to let your kids just be and trust that they can take care of themselves, because, honestly, as a child, even in Baltimore, I was one of those kids who was left alone, not in the bad way, but I was able to just be engulfed in my own imagination. Anything that I said I wanted to do, even if it sounded ridiculous or crazy, my grandma had this line she would tell me: "Everything you touch will turn to gold."

How powerful to instill that type of scripture in your child, to allow them to have that space and that carefree environment, even when they're living in a city that's plagued with an anti-black that's economically systematic. I was deep in the trenches of Baltimore and born and raised in the hood with all that shit going on in the '90s, but my mom and my grandma raised me to have my independence. And it sounds like you had a similar experience. So how does growing up in St. Croix influence the visual aesthetic of your work?

s.e.a.: You're asking the best questions. I didn't used to think about it as influencing the work I do until recently. I've been obsessed with, and it's probably from the last time I went home, which was earlier this year, I've just been obsessed with plant life, and trees, and seed pods in particular, all of these natural things that you can't necessarily get up here, and really thinking about the projects that I should be doing that I can add that island filter to.

AMA: I love that. Island filter. Because I think that, as artists, we ... part of being an artist is like you're born and obviously your DNA determines certain things about you, but so much of who you are as an artist is determined by how you grow up, the things that you see, the things that you take in and everything that affects you, in my mind, becomes a filter. When you're then making work, it's passing through all these things that you experience, right?

s.e.a.: I'm glad you get it. I think that the island-ness comes out in my photography probably more in the way that I work, in that I like to be alone and I like to have very few things. There's a minimalism to the actual work and in the way that I work.

AMA: A stillness, a peace. With the work you've done at parties or events, I do see your St. Croix experience and how you were raised show up in that work as well.

s.e.a.: Really? Tell me how.

AMA: For one, you were allowed to be this carefree child, right? And I feel like that's why you maybe are attracted to moments of joy and people in celebration of joy and love and intimacy. And I also feel like, even though I guess there's no intentional color composition in that work, it's not like a studio or like a stage shoot, but I do see those shots being colorful as well. Not just with actual color but the energy and the spirit of it.

s.e.a.: I understand what you're saying exactly, and first of all, thank you. I've never thought about shooting those party scenes in that way—that I've come from this carefree place so I am attracted to joy and I'm attracted to that carefree nature and my eye would naturally go to that. It makes sense and you're so right about that.

    And then the second part, the colorful. I was thinking about this as you were asking me about whether or not being raised on an island influences my work. I, for the most part, dream in black and white. When I'm shooting, I see it in my head as black and white. When I'm shooting in digital, I have my camera set on the black and white setting, even though I know those pictures are going to be color. I want to compose the scene, and whether that's something staged, or even when I'm out catching that moment, there's still an element of composition with that, and for me colors distract me from the composition part of it. The wonderful thing about shooting something like Joy or Laid, is they're both just so colorful. They're colorful parties in the people that come and how they present themselves and everything. When I then go back and edit these pictures all of those colors are exactly what they're supposed to be in that moment. It just works.

AMA: What is the first image that you really were like, "Oh, this is it . . ."

s.e.a.: The woman that I shot for the 13 Years of Freedom project.

AMA: I love those photos.

s.e.a.: Those pictures are, and still to this day, about as close as I've come to making what I'm seeing in my head a reality.

AMA: Let's get into those photos.

s.e.a.: That was my girlfriend at the time. She had been growing her dreads probably about nine, ten years when we got together. She had a fucked-up childhood, she's from Detroit, just all kinds of badness. Really, really bad shit. And she got out and had this boyfriend in a band that was doing very well, and they went out to L.A. He went to get a hot dog at Pink's, and some dude was trying to do a gang initiation and ran up and slit his throat, and he died.

So she came from this horribleness to being sort of rescued and on this great track to having that all just ripped away and the person that she loved just senselessly murdered. She kind of lost it a little bit, and the only thing that was keeping her grounded was she started twisting her hair. She started growing these dreads. I used to oil them and twist them—they were extremely heavy. And we would talk about the roots of the actual locs. They were started from this really horrific place of pain, and every time she would go through something that was traumatic, she would twist her hair and loc up her hair.

Her ends had started to break off, which happens, especially when you've been wearing your locs for a long time, and one of them had broken off, and I cut it open a little bit and they were black inside.

Like, they had almost carbonized the hair. If you know anything about locs, and I'm sure you do, it's a spiritual connection.

And not only that, it's a body modification if you're doing it right. You are putting time and energy and intention into something that you can then manipulate in a lot of ways. So, anyway, all this stuff. And then one day she said, "I'm going to cut them off—I think it's time for me to let go of all of this negativity and pain that I've been putting in my hair all these years." And I said, "I agree with you, I think you should. And I think that you should do something to commemorate this and not just cut them off and be done with it."

And the moment I said that, I got a picture of her. She was also a dom and in the world of kink, and I had teased her one day. I said, "Oh, your hair's long enough that I could tie you up with it," and my mind went right back to that. I said, "Let's do this project before you cut your hair. We'll tie you up with your hair." It's just like how bondage can be. It is something traumatic that can also, then, using this bondage, release from that pain.

She said, "OK." I was very lucky that she's that person that was like, "OK, I trust you and let's do it."

AMA: And they came out really good. I mean, powerful. You feel the energy in the photos. Whatever energies you're carrying and whatever you materialize is really transmuted within the photos, and it's a very visual experience.

So these Polaroids actually feature someone with no hair. I want to know more about the Polaroid pictures, because they're beautiful. Especially the one with the sticks as a crown.

s.e.a.: Oh, the willow branches.

AMA: Yes, the willow branches. It gives very much so alien, but like not. I don't know, it feels just otherworldly.

s.e.a.: I've been a lump creatively this whole pandemic. And I started thinking about what are the things that are making me happy right now and what can I do creatively that's not going to require a whole bunch of work. If I'm shooting digitally, then I have to set up the lights and shoot and then put them on the computer and edit them and da da da. So I decided, let me just make it really easy on myself—I'll just shoot Polaroids. Can't adjust it, it is what it is. I will either be happy with it or I won't. And what else is making me happy? Well, nature and my little garden. I have a little tiny studio apartment and I have roof access, so I have a little garden up there, thank God.

I found these willow branches at a farmer's market and stripped them all down. And I spray-painted them gold. I just want to play with stuff. I want to just be tangible, because I've been missing the darkroom, missing touching things. I like making things. And I have also been, obviously, in this time, thinking about Octavia Butler. I've re-read the parables again. I've read them like six times. And I'm thinking that would be really kind of beautiful if I could create this crown that would emulate that and … how do I do all of this and not spend a ton of money? Luckily, I have a beautiful girlfriend who is down for crazy ideas. And then I started just running around, like why am I buying stuff when I can ride around the neighborhood, get some exercise, and some air, and find stuff to shoot?

I found so many cool things, the seed pods. Our friends have a willow tree, and I'm going to go over there and cut some more willow branches and make some more things out of it, because it's just really beautiful.

AMA: And I see, again, St. Croix showing up in these photos.

s.e.a.: Yeah, connecting with all of that nature, finding these trees, these wonderful seed pods, the flamboyant tree and all of that.

AMA: I really see in everything that you do—this beautiful intimacy, all the photos, even the Laid photos, even your in-the-field photos, there's that intimacy, no matter how much your camera costs or whatever classes you took, photography or whatever you watch on YouTube, you can't get that skill and that eye. You have to be searching for that intimacy and want that within your work.

s.e.a.: I don't like to run out and just shoot people. I like to know something about somebody, I like to have conversations. I always want somebody to be able to trust me enough to know that I'm going to make you as beautiful as you possibly can be through the way that I see you. That's my goal. That's why editing, for me, takes forever, especially party stuff, because I look through every face, and I want to make sure that nobody looks hideous.

AMA: That is care.

s.e.a.: I think it's important, especially for us black, brown, queer people. We see so much pain, we experience so much pain from the outside world. And I can come from the inside being black, being queer, and have this just natural trust. Because I am you, you are me. I see how you are, you see how I am. You're in a safe place. I'm not going to make you look bad. I'm not here to exploit you.

Honestly, there's this little internal battle when I shoot parties. I don't want the rest of the straight world to see it a lot of the time. I really wish sometimes that I could just keep these pictures that I take for the queer community. I almost think, like, straight people, you don't deserve to see how we really get down, how we really are with each other.

AMA: It's a privilege for them to see us in that type of space. When they do see us as our most fullest self, sometimes it can come off as voyeuristic, in a negative way.

s.e.a.: A hundred percent. When I go to these parties, I'm not that nightlife photographer who's, oh, it's Friday night and I'm stopping off at your party and your party and your party and your party. When I go to a party, I'm there for *that* party. And I'm smoking my weed, I'm drinking my shots in the back, I'm dancing, I'm in the middle of the crowd. I'm there to have a good time too, because that party is for me too.

AMA: Yeah, so let me say this. I'm a music artist and I performed a bunch of times, everywhere. Honestly, the photos you took for the Laid party that I DJed at are some of my favorite performance photos of all time. I remember when those photos came out, we all just were so excited to see them. You capture all of us just having so much fun, joy, the smiles on our faces, the movement in the photos, you captured that joy and that love that we were all living and swimming in that night. Honestly one of the best parties I ever DJed at. It was a wonderful night.

We were so pressed to put the photos out there, and I remember everyone was sharing those photos because it was so good, and I really thank you for that, and I see that. As a photographer and as an artist, you really use care as a practice. You use joy as a practice. It's not like this feeling that you're trying to seek, it's really like a philosophy, a religion. The Laid party, and all the party photos—they feel like portraits. They feel like portraits versus event photography, like you were speaking to. You really get into someone's being and soul. From the Polaroid shots, or the Thirteen Years of Freedom to the party photography, even though they are all different situations, the access of your eye and your cadence is universal in all of it.

s.e.a.: I think about this a lot, actually.

As to the nightlife and party stuff versus the studio stage stuff, I've always battled myself with it. Until probably about 2011, I wasn't really thinking about it in the sense of documentation and representation. Because a lot of it was just a job, or I'm out anyway so why not take some pictures? I really fought it, really, really hard. I thought, "No. I'm an artist. I can do the stage stuff and have these wonderful photographs. This nightlife stuff, anybody—any old person can do it." And once I started looking at other nightlife photography, I realized, "No, not anybody, *you* can do this, and people want your pictures because *you* do give that joy and it's not just like regular old pictures."

And then I started wishing I had been shooting more—because I was present during the late '90s and early 2000s—of this intense gay party scene that nobody has pictures of. Nobody. It was so underground and nobody was shooting it. I beat myself up about it now. I think that it's so important for me to create this record of us being joyful, being beautiful.

AMA: I get very emotional when I think about my black LGBTQ elders and ancestors from the '80s and '90s. So much of their work was lost because of the AIDS and HIV thing. When I'm doing research or when I'm trying to look back into the archives, there's literally nothing there to find. And I know there was so much black queer talent in the '80s and '90s, especially for art and fashion and everything creative. And I think it's important for us to just document our experiences right now.

s.e.a.: I think about when I first came to New York, it was '93, and I started working in the clubs as a door person, in '95, '96. I think about how many people are gone, not even because of AIDS, but because they just died. How many people have died because of the coronavirus? How many people are just gone? And none of that nightlife has been documented at all. And I know, because I was there keeping people out that had cameras, because it was supposed to be that place where you really could be as free as you wanted, because we, the people at the door, were going to keep you safe.

They were coming from that club era of super-underground, super-secret, to the '80s, then the AIDS epidemic, to a place where you could come out. You could be fabulous. But it was in these really specific places, ball culture and all of that stuff. There is so little footage: video footage or photography. And I think to myself, I could have been the one documenting. I could have asked, "Can I shoot this?" And maybe they would have said, "Oh yeah, sure, no problem."

Those parties don't exist anymore. Like, first of all, big club parties don't even really exist . . .

AMA: Oh, that culture is gone.

s.e.a.: It's gone. And now even little club stuff is gone with the 'rona. We're doing these Zoom parties, but it's not the same, and what is the future of parties going to look like? It's giving me so much anxiety to think about. Like, am I really going to go out to a party with a thousand people and think I'm going to be safe? I don't know, but I miss it. I don't know.

AMA: Mm-hmm. Yeah, I feel you on that.

s.e.a.: But yeah, honestly, this has inspired me a lot—the idea of how important it is to actually document. There's not that much out there, and even though we have gay marriage, we have more queer and trans people on TV, I still feel a lot of the systematic violence that's going on.

AMA: But also, I feel like we aren't actually embracing our stories, and our stories still aren't seen as important to document on the front lines of media and everything, unless it's like trauma porn or unless we are the shiny object in a heteronormative piece. There's still a lot of work to be done.

s.e.a.: And I think that's where you come in, that's where I come in, that's where our artists come in and let us tell our own stories, because when you're having somebody white and straight and cis tell this story, they're putting . . . we're talking about filters, they're putting it through that filter. And while that might explain it for somebody just like them, for me it reads as false and it reads as exploitative. It reads as you're just looking at zoos and animals in the zoo. You're not really understanding who and what I am.

That's why we create our own stories. There's so little of our history for us to access, but we're here and we exist with the little bit of knowledge that we had of our past, right? So imagine if we have all of this now at our disposal to really document, to really have this catalog of images, of videos, of experiences for that next generation to build on. Imagine the platform that we give them to stand on. I think it's so important for us to document all of our stuff. All of it, all of it, all of it.

AMA: It is. It is. It is. It's very important for us to have these conversations and to have these dialogues, and to write about each other and interview each other and put them in print. It's been such a blessing to talk about you and learn about your history.

s.e.a.

13 Years of Freedom No. 1, 2007
Polaroid Type 55 Platinum print
6" x 9"

13 Years of Freedom No. 2, 2007
Polaroid Type 55 Platinum print
6" x 9"

s.e.a.

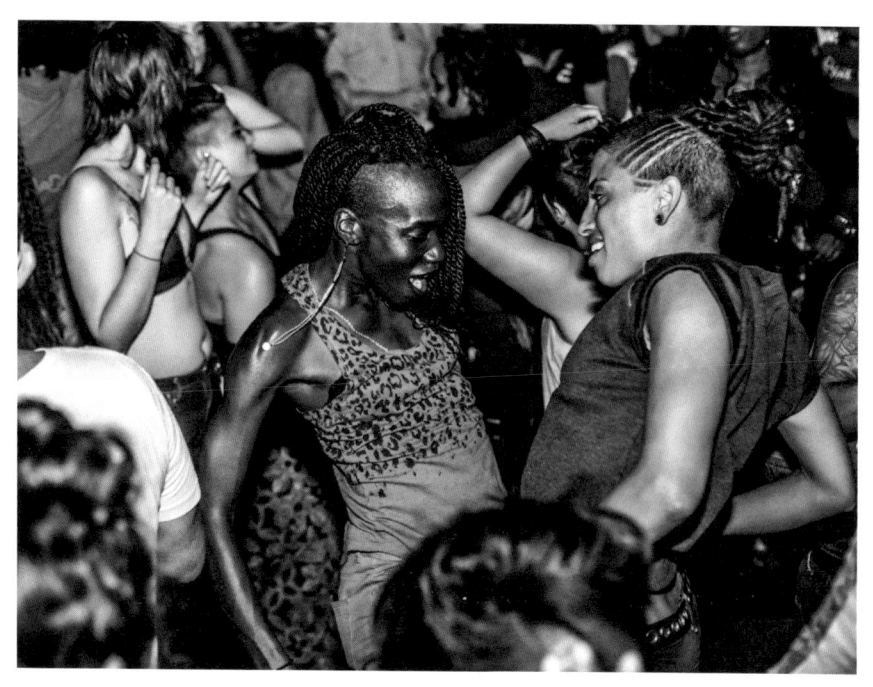

Set It Off: Queer Hip Hop Party, 2015
Digital Photograph 11" x 17"

LAID Queer Dance Party, 2019
Digital Photograph, 11" x 17"

JOY Party BK: Black August, 2018
Digital Photography 11" x 17"

JOY Party BK: PRIDE, 2018
Digital Phtograph, 11" x 17"

s.e.a.

Orlando in Black, 2020
SX-70 balck & white Polaroid
4.2" x 3.5"

Lush, 2020
SX-70 black & white Polaroid
4.2" x 3.5"

s.e.a.

The Dark, 2020
SX-70 black & white Polaroid
4.2" x 3.5"

ALYSSA CRUZ

Bedhog

my bald head & i have shared a bed for twelve years—
she prefers flat pillows, velvet sheets, and the comforter

up to her earlobes. she tugs my wrist to follow along her
nighttime routine: *don't look in the mirror to brush your
teeth, sit on the floor with your back against the sink.*

when i start to feel lonely, she instructs me to press
the cabinet's knob against the back of her ear and feel

the silver's coolness. it's her way of reminding me,
i am in her orbit. she controls my gravity. i tilt to her.
she's a starfish sleeper, wakes up to her own snores.

she can't fall asleep in hotels unless she's on her left side
and facing the wall. she promises someday she'll let me

have sleepovers that don't end in us tiptoeing out at 2 AM.
over breakfast, i asked her when we'll be ready to wake up
to someone new. she kept chewing her toast and shrugged,

*when someone knows to sit cross-legged beside us,
without needing to understand why.*

Something Quite Big

"You smell like coyotes," says the son to his father. "Like one coyote or the whole pack?" queries the father. "It depends on the size of the pack. No more than fourteen, but certainly no fewer than four," says the son. "Have they killed anything of late?" asks the father. "Why yes, they have just now killed something," the son answers. The father sniffs himself. "It was big, wasn't it?" he asks. "Oh yes, they have just now killed something quite big," says the son. "But it's just now been killed?" asks the father. "Yes, just moments ago. The big thing was alive and with his family less than an hour before our conversation," decides the son. "Well that's not so bad then, since it's not had time to decay. I feel better," said the father, turning into a number of coyotes and bursting out the screen door. The son stands at the door, counting.

SOPHIA TARIN

The Mute Button

I had no   in the beginning, longer than was expected.
Someone stole my   .
My mouth opened and I didn't know how to   language.
People would   to me.
It was as decipherable as the song of a bird in a tree.
I was starved for   .
I was aching for communication.
          to say *chair*   *sit*
I knew   what was, but   not in language.
I lacked the   word for *cucumber* till high school.
I called it *baud rang*.
Is that a   word?
What do you mean my   is scary?
It's Persian for   .
Can I coat aggressive words with feminine endings?
Is it the French or am I dyslexic?
          to say *Septembre*   *Bleu*.
My sentences were   .
I was   the full vocabulary like trying
to finish a puzzle with the   pieces.

Brave Iguana People Only Love Acid Rain

I remember how your car told me I wasn't safe in its belly. How it was so hot outside that the metal from the seatbelt scorched my palm. How your air freshener swung like a pendulum when the vehicle bobbed out of the driveway and into the street. How the sky was so perfect that it looked like we were in the final scene of a 1970s musical where the camera would pan up and curly yellow letters would form "The End" and people watching in the theater would clap their hands and laugh as the projector spilled dusty light over their heads. I remember feeling grateful that you were taking me to the library because you were always my favorite cousin.

I remember how we never made it to the library.

I remember digging through my backpack for that pencil you asked for and hearing something roll around the carpet floor as we turned a corner. How you asked what I was working on in math and I said "factoring." How you said we might as well get some work done on the car ride there anyway, right?

How you abruptly turned your head to me and murmured that you were going to write a symphony. I couldn't tell anybody because you said it was a secret. I laughed because you sounded creepy and besides you never played any instruments except Guitar Hero and the occasional finger drumming on your leg and how I just wanted to know if I should distribute before adding or should I wait to do it afterwards. But you looked at me with glassy eyes and didn't turn your head even though the car was moving and the world was whipping in colors of green and yellow and blue behind you. You told me it didn't matter that you couldn't read music and that I was just like everyone else who said you couldn't do something. I remember the way the trees recoiled in fear and covered their eyes when they saw your car headed straight for them.

I remember the way my shoes sounded when they scuffed the floor of the mechanic shop in Costco. How we waited in line until your dad came and said it was OK. It was OK. These things happen you know. But his eyes said, *Get it together, kid. What are you doing? Such a failure. You're not listening to me. Look at me. What a failure.* How he rubbed his hand across his face because these things couldn't happen anymore.

What a failure.

How your mom made me a cinnamon bun and asked me if I was hurt. How the icing made my fingers stick to the math test and I told her I wasn't hurt.

How you told her to get out of the room because you knew how to tutor and she was distracting you.

How the puppet of your soul sprung to life and the marionettist flipped a switch in your brain. How another version of you started to scare me because it held up my test and screamed in my face and banged its fist on the table and asked why I got a 39%. How it tilted its head and its eyes said, *Such a failure. You're not listening to me. Look at me. What a failure.* How you rubbed your hand across your face because these things couldn't happen anymore.

What a failure.

But most of all, I remember how terrified I was because someone I loved wanted to hurt me. How I didn't recognize you anymore. How you weren't the cousin who made cannolis with me and held my hand when I got my ears pierced. How I left your house and almost collapsed out the front door because you were only a stranger.

I remember how mom's car told me I was safe in its belly. How the seatbelt hugged me and said you're okay. How I bit my lip and tried so hard not to cry but failed at that too. How tears spilled down my face and blurred my vision into kaleidoscope diamonds. And she stopped the car and said you're scaring me you're scaring me what happened Maddy tell me right now. And my lips were glued together and my head hung and I told her that something was wrong with you. How I didn't know you anymore. How I thought you were on drugs. How I was so scared. How you were insane.

How strange the word "bipolar" sounded to all of us.

How your name became a secret that everyone prodded with a stick and backed away from.

How I was angry.

How I really miss you.

PETE FORTENBAUGH

Inheritance

"Ain't no way you can burry him under that house. Ain't no way. Yer pap-pap was crazier'an hellfire toward the end. Everbody knowed that."

"Welp, I promised it to him," the boy said.

The boy's great-uncle stood there scratching his old black lab's ear and shaking his head in the early morning sun. "But he was crazier'an hell-fire," Roger said. "Gowan: ask any soul on the island. Nobody'd put no stock in nothing he said no more."

"Don't make no diffrence if he were crazy or not. I promised it to him, and that's all there is to it."

"You don't owe him a thing. He's got him a plot in Cambridge that Darlene and I paid for. They'll dig'er with a excavator and that's it. Funeral home'll organize it and dress him and everthing."

The boy stood there staring across the island and the bay beyond, his jaw set as straight as the horizon. "You know as well as me, he tolt ever soul that'd listen not to let them bury him off a this island. And to put him in the ground right under that house if there weren't no other place that'd have him."

"But ye don't owe a dead man nothin. He's got him a place all set aside in Cambridge. Ain't like it makes a bit a diffrence to him now."

"Look, Uncle Roger, I ain't got time for this. If ye don't wanta lend me that hand spade, I'll find one somewheres else."

"Awright, awright; I'll get'er for ye. But you know it don't make no diffrence." Roger limped off around the corner of his house, around back to the outhouse, where he kept his gardening tools. His dog followed at his heel and he mumbled to it as he went, "Cain't talk common sense to them that ain't got none. Never heard nothin so crazy in all m'life."

The boy stayed in the front yard with his foot on the front step of his great-uncle's big house on West Water Street. He fingered a cigarette and a lighter out of his coat pocket, lit the cigarette, and looked up at the sky. It was November and the heavens were as clear and dry as a pane of glass. The sun had been up an hour; it was hollow-white: more cold than hot. He shivered and thought how miserable, muddy, and wet it was going to be underneath the house. His pap-pap's brother came stumping back around the corner of his house, holding a hand spade and a nice, new, full-length shovel.

"Don't need the shovel. Pap-Pap's got one."

"Take it anyhow. I know what his tools is worth."

The boy took the shovel grudgingly, hating to admit what he knew to be true. "I'll bring'er by when I'm done," he said, and started off towards the little house on Sun Street.

"Me and Darlene'll be by within the hour to get him cleaned up and dressed."

The boy kept walking.

His pap-pap's house, where they both lived, had about the smallest plot of land on the whole island of Johnsontown. The entire walk along Sun Street, the boy kept his eyes on the slumping little building. The house was two stories and had four windows facing the street. Chain-link fences were elbow-close on both sides. Over the years, the phragmites had crept right up to the back step like a hungry herd of cats, and the whole building seemed to be leaning back onto its heels from where it had settled into the marsh. There was only a three-foot strip of front yard, and that was mostly occupied by two half-dead cedar bushes that scratched at the house when the wind blew west.

Their neighbor, a sun-dried, old black woman named Dot Johnson, was leaning on her chain-link fence, so close she could've reached out and touched the chimney of the old man's house.

"I'm sorry Noah," she said when the boy got close enough, "Mr. Ham was as good a man as I'm ever knowed, Christian or not."

"Nothin to be sorry about. He's getting the onliest thing he wanted."

"So you's gonna do it like he sayed?"

"It's the onliest thing I can do."

"The Good Lord don't forget them that bear the cross. He be smiling down on you." Then, when the boy didn't respond, she said, "Just knock on the door when ye get hungry, now."

"Thank ye, mam," he said. She watched him as he emptied his pockets of everything but his cigarettes, his lighter, and the old man's blue metal flashlight. Then he got down on his stomach and crawled through the gap in the cinderblock foundation at the back of the house.

It was wet under there like he knew it would be. There was only about two feet of space between the underbelly of the house and the oily, black mud. He put the flashlight in his mouth, his teeth clamping down on the cold textured metal, and then he started belly-crawling through the muck, shovel in one hand, spade in the other. He shimmied his way toward the far front corner of the house, where the ground was the highest.

The bluish light of the flashlight wagged back and forth as he wove his way along, doing his best to miss the puddles where the last of the year's mosquito larva danced in flicking spurts of mud. Old, broken glass and rusty metal caught the light. Mold-blackened insulation hung down like peeled-back fur. Spider webs grabbed at his hair and ears. Everything smelled like stagnant water mixed with sewage, decay, and rot.

He wondered how in the Hell he was going to get the old man and his box through all of this, but he remembered what the old man always said: "Damn right it can be done, and that's just how she's got to be done." No sooner had he thought this thought than a rusty nail from a floor joist scraped his scalp. He opened his mouth in shock and pain. The flashlight fell and rolled away into a puddle. It went out, leaving him in a sudden darkness. He cursed and felt about blindly. His hand touched something hard and furry that didn't feel like insulation. He recoiled and fumbled for his cigarette lighter. When he lit it, its shaking orange light revealed the shrunken, eyeless form of a mummified cat. He felt a wave pass through his body; it took a second before he moved. The lighter burned his fingers and went out, and he thought: sometimes it's better not to see, and then he crawled on around the cat, towards the far corner of the house.

The ground was dry there, but there was less space to work—little more than a foot between the dirt and the joists and pipes above. Again he heard the old man: "Damn right it can be done, and that's just how she's got to be done," and so he stabbed the blackness with the spade. It was easier once the work began, and he found he didn't miss the light.

"Time ain't the same under a house," the old man used to say when they did plumbing jobs together. And it was true too. The digging was hard because after the first few inches of soft soil, the boy hit hard-packed oyster shell that cut his knuckles as he hacked away with the spade. He could picture the old man under there with him perfectly: grunting as he lay on his back, smearing purple plumber's cement on busted pipes with that smell that made your head feel light and heavy at the same time. "Sometime you come out from a house crawl and she's gettin dark, and othertimes it ain't even lunch time yet." The boy could hear the old man saying it as they worked together in the mud. "God-damn I hate a God-damn house crawl," he'd say. But still, when pipes on the island busted or a new bathroom was being put in, the old man was who everyone on the island called.

And he'd do it every time, even up until nearly the end when he couldn't hardly move his knees and had to stop and catch his breath every 30 seconds. He could never turn them down.

The boy heard footsteps on the floor above his head. Darlene was wearing heels.

"How ye doin under thare?" Uncle Roger's head was sticking through the opening in the cinderblock foundation at the back of the house. "What, ain't ye got no light?"

"Fell in a puddle."

"Want me to pass one to ye?"

"I'm fine. You get used to it."

"Suit yerself." Roger snuffled and coughed. "Anything else ye need?"

"No."

His great-uncle stayed there with just his head poking under. Then he said, "Awright. Darlene's getting Ham's suit on him." The boy kept digging, grunting each time he drove the spade in the hard, packed shell. "You sure we can get him and that box all the way through to ye o'er there?"

"He built that box special. He knowed how high to make'er."

"Yeah, I imagine he did." Roger lingered a few minutes longer, and then said again, "Darlene's getting him dressed. Give a holler if ye need anything."

Despite what he wanted, the boy found himself imagining what was going on just above his head, in the old man's bedroom beside the kitchen: Darlene stripping the old man naked and cleaning him up. Sliding his stiff legs into his only suit and cinching that black string tie up around the old man's bulging Adam's apple. The boy had found the old man in bed that morning when he'd come in to help the old man to the bathroom. It had been pretty much liked he'd imagined it would be, except that the old man's cataract-clouded eyes and toothless mouth were open. That was the hardest part: it meant he wasn't sleeping when he passed. The boy wondered if the old man had called and he hadn't heard him through his sleep, and then the boy felt an exhaustion that was nearly too heavy to bear.

"Don't gimme no church service," he could hear the old man saying. "Let them Christians keep their damned judgment and redemption to theirselfs." For the last three months, since the stroke had cut the old man in two, it was all he wanted to talk about. "I know Roger wants to take me off the island to that cemetery in Cambridge, just cause they won't have me in their God-damned churchyard. You see to it that I'm in the ground under my house if they ain't no other place. That's all that matters. You hear me? I'm tolt Roger how I want it. And that you be the one's in charge. He knows it, and he ain't gonna like it none, but God-damnit, when this whole fuckin island's under water I wanta be here with her." The spade slipped and an oyster shell sliced a scallop into his pinky finger.

"God-damn-it all," he cursed, and he heard Darlene's footsteps pause above his head. God-damn-it, he'd curse if he god-damn-well pleased.

"Yer word's all yer got and you gotta live so everbody knows what ye say is what ye do. It ain't how ye pray, it's how ye live. That's what all these God-damned so-called Christians on this island don't see, the way they cheat and steal and talk behind yer back." It was a rant the boy had heard from the old man since that first night he'd come to stay, 10 long year ago. He'd knocked on his pap-pap's front door after walking 22 miles from Cambridge, carrying nothing but a backpack with one set of clothes, a couple comics, and a tattered blue blanket he'd always slept with. The old man had opened the door like he'd been waiting for him, fully dressed despite the hour. "I knowed they couldn't keep ye off the island," he'd said, putting his hand on the boy's head, heavy as an anchor.

The boy's mother had come after him the next morning, and the three of them had sat there in the parlor, the old man blowing smoke in his mother's face and drinking his beer. "Cambridge ain't no place for an island boy. If he's got the mud tween his toes they ain't nothing you can do to keep him off." After two hours of arguing, she'd agreed to let the boy stay. She'd said then that she was trying to convince her new husband, Jake, to buy a house on Johnsontown so they could be together, but the boy knew that that was more of his mother's talk about things that wouldn't never happen.

The hole was deep enough now that the boy could use the shovel. He was still on his stomach, but it was easier and it went a little faster. He was careful to heap the dirt on the far side of the hole, banked against the foundation, so it wouldn't interfere when it was time to slide the box in. "Do things right and you'll always have work. This island needs people can fix things. Long as you can fix whatever's broke, and you do things right, yer gonna have more work'an you can handle." He taught the boy how to fix engines, pipes, rot; how to build steps, lay carpet, frame and drywall. The old man had dropped out of school at 13, yet he knew more than most people, more than the boy's mother or her husband Jake with their college educations.

The boy had dropped out at 17 and started working full-time with his pap-pap because, by then—though he'd never admit it—the old man couldn't do it all on his own any longer. Water started filling the bottom of the boy's hole, and he wasn't even three foot down.

"Noah, honey, how you doin down thare?" his mother's voice called from the opening in the foundation.

"Fine."

"We're making lunch if you wanna take a break."

"I be out when I'm done."

She stayed there at the opening, like Uncle Roger had done. None of them could let him be. "It's noon. People'll be showing up in two more hours."

"I'll be done by then."

"Make sure you have time to get cleaned up."

"You don't think I know that?"

"Awright, honey, awright. There's a plate for you when you get out."

He crawled out something like an hour later and stood there in the sun, smoking a cigarette, muddy and wet from head to toe. He picked the dirt from the cuts on his hands and noted with appreciation that the day was warmer than it had been in a week. A low-flying flock of newly arrived geese came honking over the island and he heard the old man's delighted cry: "Dead gooses!"

Inside they'd draped the kitchen table in someone's navy-blue bedsheet, and the old man was on top of it in that strangely shallow box that he'd built out of unpainted yellow pine. They'd got his eyes and mouth to close, and combed his beard and got him into his only suit—the one he had just for funerals. That made the boy laugh out loud, and his mother and his Uncle Roger and Aunt Darlene looked at him funny, but he didn't say a word and went straight to the bathroom for a quick shower.

Pretty much all 438 people on the island showed up by 2 p.m., flooding Sun Street and Loblolly in both directions. They'd brought the kitchen table out onto the front porch, and the old man lay there sort of grinning like the joke was on them. Even though it wasn't what the old man wanted, Reverend Joshua gave a drawn-out speech: about how the old man was stubborn and opinionated as a man could be, but how there weren't a soul on the island that didn't love him dearly for the good works he did day in and day out; how the loss of any one islander was a loss to them all; and how, as Reverend Joshua said, he was sure there was a place in the Kingdom of Heaven for a man such as that. The boy found himself chewing on his tongue, thinking how except for the few like Dot Johnson and his mother on the weekends, the island had left it up to him and him alone to care for the old man in his hour of need. The boy stood there on the porch, in front of them all in his own shabby funeral suit, and he didn't say a word. Then there was the moment where they all sang *Amazing Grace*, and again the boy laughed out loud, hearing the old man say, "God-damned Methodists sing like a crooked record."

They put the lid on, and the boy himself nailed it shut, clearly seeing the old man's smiling face straight through the wood every time the hammer came down. The tears came then, and it all seemed so wrong, leaving him there in a wet hole under a dark house. But again he heard the old man saying, "Damn right it can be done, and that's just how she's got to be done," and him and three others, Uncle Roger, Danny Pinder, and Booger Jr. (serving in Booger Sr.'s stead), carried the old man around to the opening in the foundation at the back of the house. The boy hadn't expected them to, but all three of them—even old Uncle Roger and Danny with that gut of his— squeezed under the old man's house in their church clothes to help him drag the old man and his box all the way to the far corner where the boy's hole was waiting.

Danny held the flashlight and together, on their stomachs, they angled the box down into the hole where it splashed into the wet bottom. Then all together, using the shovel, the spade and their hands, they covered the old man up.

"Lord I hope he don't come floatin back up," Danny said as the other three men worked.

"He figured on that," the boy said. "He drilt a bunch a holes in the bottom of the box so tide can come and go."

"Lord have mercy," Danny said.

"He ain't want to be here none did he?" Booger Jr. laughed.

When the dirt was all humped and packed as best they could, Uncle Roger said, "He arta be happy now." Then, "Yer done good, Noah."

"It's what I owed him," the boy said without looking at the others.

"Yeah, yer done good, awright," Uncle Roger said. "I still cain't believe it, but yer done it, and it's more'an anybody but him coulda asked."

Each of the older men silently put their hands on the boy between them, and then Booger Jr said, "Lord it's nastier'an Hell under here. Let's get back out into the sunshine."

That afternoon, after everybody'd left and the boy had showered once again, he went into the old man's room. Sunlight was slanting through the western window onto the old man's bed in a golden kind of way. Dust moved in the light as if the air itself were alive. For some reason—the boy couldn't say why—he lay down for the first time in the bed where he'd found the old man that very same morning. He could smell him in the sheets, and the sun was so warm, like it was holding him in a divine embrace, and he realized that this was all his now, his inheritance, this gravestone of a house, and it was up to him to keep on living it, and then he drifted off into something deeper than sleep.

MISCHELLE ANTHONY

The Heart Is Difficult to Know

We hold no illusions of rising again,
witness instead the six-man struggle
to carry the dead across. It's
underneath when finally
the sheen is sanded off. Watch out
for splinters. Time doesn't care
for the tender skin, its ever-
deepening lines on the palm.
And the undertaker never gets
the mouth just right.
Lips press and sag.

Sure as alfalfa wilt in the afternoon, death
should unleash a circus of grief, its garish
ribbons embossed like money
clips with initials, nicknames, and kin.
Don't get stuck in the ripping apart,
loss like shaggy biscuit dough,
body burned to powder, flotsam
on the sea. Who doesn't need a stone
reminder craned into the squared-
off earth? Grass bows above exhausted
roots, patient as the gentle wear
that changes skin to bone.

They didn't remove
my mother's heart
before the formaldehyde
went in. It wisened like an apple
in June's dark pantry or a lemon
left out too long. I imagine it
now curled in on itself,
another fist bracing against
the darkness we must face.

CATHERINE-ESTHER COWIE

Still Singing Even Without Faith in the Universe

after Brittney Scott

1
In one, she has options, lets the doctor
take the newly formed baby flesh.
Keeps it a secret like the gold bangles
hidden behind the dresser—a gift
from her sister's husband.
He pays for the procedure. Stops touching her.

She knifes out a place in a different village,
a small room with a view of the sea.
Attaches herself to an Englishman.
When drunk, he beats her.

Pregnant with her fifth, ladling ginger tea
in cups for the other three, who has time
to mourn? To imagine the look of the first child,
blonde and tanned like the father, boy or girl,
to imagine grandchildren, and great-grands,
to imagine me—

In another universe, she fights him off.
And in another, her nephews and nieces
happen upon them on the kitchen floor. He stops.
In both she escapes to her mother's, refuses to return.
Spends her days washing clothes in the river.
Eating mangoes. Walking home
towards the village, a man drags her
into the bushes, forces her.

In some universes, we don't exist,
cut off in bloom or never taking root.
In few, she chooses not to stay with the men who abuse her.
In each, she knows her body as bruised and broken into.

2
Do I praise biology's apathy in this universe—
a bloodline spun and replicating
from a young woman's pain and a man's pleasure?

Dare I believe that some invisible force's hand
insisted on this child's life,
flesh and blood webbing
into tiny hands, tiny feet—my Grandma.
Same hand that refused to intervene.

What then do we call ourselves,
children blossoming from a wound?
Do we live in fear of the shadow
careening through our blood?
Listen closely to the movement
of our hands, listen for their itch
to break another?

3
I bless you Great-grandma,
press a fingertip of olive oil to your forehead.
Lace hibiscus and marigold through your hair.
Kiss your cheeks. Knead coconut
oil into the ash of your back.
Bless you Great-grandma, I live.
Knew the soft of your daughter's
billowing belly. Learned later of her rage.
I live, bless you Great-grandma,
know my mother's singing,
bending me into flight, bird, into scatter.
Know her wounding.

4
If I am memory,
if I am witness,
if I speak,
let it be like a song
of those before—
their gagged speech, cry,
becoming jazz, becoming blues,
becoming calypso.
Let it be beauty tearing through
sorrow, darkening my hands,
my tongue, singing—

BRIANA MALEY

Hummingbird

You are in the fifth-grade hallway, like you always are. Mrs. Kopec says you can't sit still. Mrs. Kopec says you need to get it together. Mrs. Kopec says this is your Last Chance. Next stop, principal's office.

You don't know why you can't sit still. You don't know why you're the worst boy in the class. You don't know why you are *prone to outbursts*. That's what Mrs. Kopec wrote in the comments section of your last report card. You don't know why you let your ruler hang halfway off your desk and use it to catapult crumpled paper. You don't know why you gnaw your fingernails till they bleed.

You don't know why you ripped up your chocolate milk carton today and ate it. At first you were only going to chew on it, mash the pieces between your teeth to make papery gum. Just long enough to get the chocolate taste off. But then Lucia giggled and pulled on Antonio's sleeve. Then other kids were snickering too. With everyone watching, you couldn't spit the mess into your hand, so you swallowed. That's when the laughter really took off, rising up like a parachute lifted high overhead in PE class.

You are practicing how you will act when Mrs. Kopec comes out to talk to you. You cross your arms and roll your eyes toward the ceiling, trying to look like you don't care.

That's when you see it.

It moves so fast you could miss it, but it makes a buzzing sound too. A hum. It lands on the rafter. Its throat is a splash of red. When it moves its head, it looks robotic, like an old-fashioned wind-up toy.

Your mother had a hummingbird feeder. She died when you were in third grade. There are things you don't remember, like her voice, and things that you do, like how she filled her hummingbird feeder with red sugar water she boiled on the stovetop. She never let the feeder stay empty. It takes a lot of energy to be a hummingbird. Their wings beat 70 times per second. Their hearts beat even faster. Even when holding still, they are burning up energy, burning it up from the inside.

If you burst into the classroom to tell Mrs. Kopec, she will send you straight to the principal's office. The principal will call your father. Your father has Had Enough. Your father is at his Wit's End. He doesn't even yell anymore.

The hummingbird feeder still dangles from the tree in your backyard, empty. The red plastic top and bottom have faded. You wonder how long the hummingbirds came to look for nectar before they gave up. You wonder how many of them died.

You want this hummingbird to live.

You wonder if there is any time at all between its heartbeats. You put your hand to your chest to feel your own heart. You look down at your hand. You are wearing your red windbreaker. You remember your mother standing at the stove, stirring the red nectar. She used to hold the wooden spoon to your lips. Let you slurp up the wet sweetness.

You slide out of your jacket and hold it above your head. You wave gently. The hummingbird doesn't move. Propped in the corner, you notice the janitor's mop. You grab it and drape your windbreaker over the handle. You raise it high.

You step forward. "Come on," you whisper. "It's OK."

You think it is about to trust you. If only you could get a little closer. But if you step closer, you'll be standing in front of your classroom door. There is a window in the door. Mrs. Kopec will see you. You don't want to be the kid who's always in trouble. You step back.

The hummingbird's eyes are two tiny black beads, staring at you. If you can just get close enough, it will come. You know it.

You hold your breath and ease forward, eyes locked on the bird. You try not to see what's at the edge of your vision—your classroom, the other kids. Mrs. Kopec.

The hummingbird tilts its head to one side, then the other. After a long pause, it lets go of the rafter. It hovers above the mop handle. You ease forward, holding the mop high. For once your mind is focused. Your body moves with purpose.

The classroom door clicks open.

"Mason!" Mrs. Kopec shouts. "Mason, this is your final warning!"

You run. The hummingbird doesn't have much time, and neither do you. Speeding down the hallway, you glance up over your shoulder to make sure the hummingbird is still gliding behind you, like it's a kite and you're making sure it hasn't fallen yet.

"Mason! Principal's office!"

You make it to the end of the hallway and round the corner to the school's entryway. You bolt past the big glass windows of the front office. Inside, you see the principal. When she sees you, she bolts up from her chair. You turn around to push the front door open with your back. You dip the mop handle down to get it through the doorway. You slow down just enough to make sure the little bird stays with you.

The hummingbird swoops down and passes so close that you think you feel the tiny breeze its wings make as it zips past your cheek. You feel it the way you used to still feel your mother's goodnight kisses after she had turned out the lights.

Outside, the hummingbird darts in one direction, then another. It looks so small against the sky. You drop the mop and run behind it, arms raised high. "Go," you shout. "Fly!"

You hear Mrs. Kopec and the principal yelling at you to get inside. You keep running, face to the sky.

ELIZABETH FELICETTI

Armed

My dad wasn't a hunter but owned guns. I never thought about them until after his ten-hour surgery seventeen years ago. His surgery was in California when I was a chaplain intern at a hospital in Virginia. My siblings, who all lived in Arizona like him, took turns being with him.

I went to him as soon as I could, three months after the surgery, after I finished my internship. He seemed old. Fragile. He had never talked to me this way before: "I guess Jan told you that she hid my guns."

"Yes, she told me." It was a secret. I couldn't believe he brought it up.

"I guess that would have been really selfish," he said.

I looked outside. It was hot out there, but I preferred hot to being inside talking to my father about potentially shooting himself.

"I said I guess that would have been really selfish," he repeated, teeth clenched, eyes on me. I was his daughter who wanted to be a pastor. I was supposed to know how to answer the question he wasn't asking.

I made myself look at him. *Don't cry.* I can usually hold tears back, but sometimes my nose runs anyway.

"I don't know about selfish, Daddy, but I know none of us could bear it."

I looked out the window again. He looked too. "That's what I thought," he said.

We sat with that for a while, watching the bright pink geraniums in the raised flower bed sweltering in the sun.

He broke the silence. "I wish she'd give me back my BB gun. I'm not going to off myself with a damn BB gun, and I need to keep cats away from the quail."

"I'll talk to her, Daddy," I said.

* * *

My husband, Gary, hunts. When we were dating, he had the ugliest afghan I had ever seen in his apartment, but before I pointed this out I asked, "Did your mother make you that blanket?" Just in case.

"I made it," he replied.

I was too surprised to respond. He could crochet? "My mother helped me with the colors," he added.

When we visited his parents before we were married, his dad made us venison. I pretended to like it. "It tastes like beef," his dad said.

I'd never had venison before. I'd heard how my stepmom once put some in spaghetti and served it to my older stepsiblings. It didn't go over well, so she'd never tried it with me.

After the honeymoon, I told Jan about the venison that his dad claimed tasted like beef. "Venison tastes like cheap beef," she said. She was helping me unpack and set up our first home together. Gary was away.

We came across the ugly blanket. "This has to go," she said, setting it in the donation pile.

"He made it," I explained, taking it back.

She looked at it, and then back up at me. "You're kidding," she said. "Who told you that?"

"He did!"

"And you believed him?"

The blanket had three colors. She showed me how to fold it so only two colors showed. We put it in the guest room.

That first year we were married I suggested a no-guns-in-the-house rule. Gary agreed to keep them locked up at his parents' house. His parents gave me a venison cookbook for Christmas.

* * *

Be wise as serpents and gentle as doves, orders the tenth chapter of the Gospel of Matthew.

I should have called George's former pastor as a courtesy the first time he showed up at my church with his girlfriend, but soon after that first Sunday, they invited me over to dinner. He brought up my Facebook friendship with his former pastor and asked if we had talked about him. He seemed distressed. "No," I told him. "We're friendly, but I haven't talked to her in a few months." So I didn't call her when I sent in his letter of transfer from her church. I wanted him to have a fresh slate.

I knew George was troubled because he told me. He told me about his medications and hospitalizations. He was working with a psychiatrist, so I felt safe. But he went through several jobs and would become depressed and angry. He got a new girlfriend.

* * *

My parents moved into a facility where they could get graduated levels of care. They started out in independent living. They got to keep their dog. They made friends. They played bridge and poker.

Once Dad was having trouble finding some document and didn't want Jan to know that he didn't know where it was. "Can you find it for me?" he asked when she was out. "I think it's in my office somewhere."

I went through his desk and then his wardrobe, which had several drawers. I felt something cool wrapped up in a towel. I unwrapped a gun. Were guns allowed in this place? I wrapped it and put it back in the drawer, and I don't remember if I found the document he asked me to find.

* * *

We'd been married for at least a year when I found out the truth about the blanket. I said something about the blanket or crocheting and he responded, "What are you talking about?"

"The afghan," I said. "That you crocheted."

"Do I look like I crochet?" he said.

"No," I said. "That's part of what makes it so attractive."

"I have no idea what you're talking about," he said, gently.

"The *afghan!*" I said. "In the guest room, that you made."

"Who told you that?" he said.

"You did. When we were first dating."

"And you believed me?" he said.

My image of him as a hunter who crocheted was shattered. "You said your mother helped you pick out the colors," I reminded him.

"That's the kind of detail that makes it believable," he said. "But I can't believe you believed me."

I couldn't believe this. "It's part of what makes you so complicated and compelling," I told him.

"I think I bought that thing," he said. "I love you, but I'm not going to learn how to crochet."

I donated the blanket.

A few years later, he called me on his way home from a hunting trip. "Can you make some of your venison marinade? I'm bringing fresh meat."

"My" venison marinade was from the cookbook his parents

had given me. I made the marinade but hated putting the fresh meat into it. Three days before, the meat had been a deer frolicking in the forest, and then my husband shot it dead, and now was a cool slab that I was setting in a fragrant marinade. In a moment of epiphany, I became a vegetarian. For a month.

Sometimes he hunts with a bow and arrow. He eats what he kills. It's all regulated: more deer would starve in cold winters without hunting. I know it's better to eat food he killed instead of chicken wrapped in plastic and Styrofoam from the grocery store, chickens that lived in cages, born to become our food.

Sometimes when I get called to the hospital late at night, or when I am driving home late after traveling, I see deer. They freeze and stare and I stop the car and stare back at their huge eyes and slender legs. After a moment their ears start to move, but their eyes never waver until they run.

Sometimes they don't run away. Sometimes I drive off first.

* * *

Clergy are supposed to be a non-anxious presence.

I shouldn't have gone the time that George's new girlfriend called me to say he was staying in a hotel but was out of money, and she was three hours away and all his belongings were in a moving truck. I was afraid he was going to be out on the street and might kill himself, even though he wasn't saying that. He wouldn't tell me where he was until I promised not to call the police. I paid for three more nights in the hotel from my discretionary church fund. The secretary wouldn't leave the office until I came back safely from the hotel. That weekend his girlfriend came and got him and he went away with her, hours away, and I believed I had done the right thing, even though I was scared, but the senior warden made me promise I would never do it again. I hoped George and his girlfriend would live happily ever after three hours away and never come back.

Some six months later, he came back. George is a big guy: white, at least eight inches taller than I am, and at least a hundred pounds heavier. He came back to tell me they had broken up and he would be back in town and back in church. He didn't have an appointment; he just showed up. The secretary wouldn't leave for the day until he left. I didn't close the door when he was telling me these things, and I didn't sit down. He hugged me when he left.

I didn't get scared until a couple of weeks later, when one of his ex-girlfriends texted me and told me that she didn't think the church and I realized how sick he was. She was afraid of him but wanted to warn me, she said, because I was "a woman of God."

I didn't call his former pastor until after he got mad at me because he sent me an e-mail saying he wanted to pick me up in his truck so he could drive me, he claimed, to someone in the hospital who was dying. He didn't tell me the person's name or the hospital. There was no way I was getting in a truck with him. I tried to explain everything calmly.

When I called his former pastor, I learned that she had not been afraid of him. "I should have called you though," she said.

"I should have called you, too," I assured her.

"We both could have done things differently. I hoped he was better," she said. "Still, you should know that he has firearms."

* * *

Gary had been recalled to active duty and had to travel a lot, and our dog died the same day he went back to active duty. I wondered if I would feel safer with a gun.

When my dad was bedridden, I asked him, "Should I get a gun?"

Dad opened his eyes and said, "Only if you're willing to shoot it if someone breaks in. If you don't, then you're just getting a gun for someone else to shoot you. Have you ever shot a gun?"

"Gary took me shooting once. And there was that time you took me when I was ten."

"I did not," he said. "I never took you shooting." We looked at each other, confused.

"Did you take me?" I asked Jan. She shook her head.

But I remember. I was ten. I wore a t-shirt and cut-offs. I thought the cut-offs would make me feel tougher with their rough edges. I hated cut-offs and that's the only time I ever remember wearing them. I had wire-rimmed glasses. I don't remember who took me. I assumed it was Dad and Jan. We shot at a tin can in the desert. I don't remember hitting it, which must mean I missed. I remember the gun was heavy, and loud. Shooting was hard.

My stepbrother Scott called as we talked about this, and Jan asked if he had ever taken me shooting. He said probably. When he heard I was thinking about a gun he wanted to speak to me himself. He had lots of opinions. He told me not to get a 22 because it wouldn't kill anyone.

Back in Virginia, I went to dinner with two friends who told me to get a 380, not a 22, because a 22 wouldn't kill anyone unless it was a close shot. After dinner they showed me their gun. It was cool and black. Their dog jumped off my lap when I held their gun.

* * *

About a year after his father died, Gary took me shooting. He had a rifle that belonged to his mother and told me the story about how his dad had offered to teach his mom how to shoot back when they were dating. Afterward he learned that she'd been on the rifle team in high school.

We used paper targets. I didn't hit the bullseye, but Gary said my grouping was consistent.

While he was retrieving the targets, I took the binoculars outside of the hut we shot from and saw a grayish-brown bird with a yellow belly and black mask like a bandit, yellow tip on its tail. I grabbed my bird book and looked it up: a cedar waxwing, my first.

"Check out this bird," I said. This was shortly after I had started keeping a bird list. I was grateful he only shot deer, not birds.

* * *

Philippians tells us not to worry about anything, but in prayer and supplication with thanksgiving make our requests to God.

I didn't call my bishop about George. I called the guys in my church who have guns. I knew other clergy would be horrified. One of the men looked me in the eye and said, "I don't want you to be scared in your own church."

But I felt scared in my own church. I also felt like a bad Christian. I stood in front of the congregation armed with only a prayer book, and when George was there, I watched him throughout the service for signs that he was on his medicine. I watched him during the sermon to see if something I said made him mad. He usually looked out the window. In the greeting line, when he was there, I kept my prayer book in front of me so he wouldn't hug me.

We had a clergy conference shortly after the shooting in Sutherland Springs, Texas. The presiding bishop was there. I felt like we were at a bobblehead conference because we all nodded at everything he said. Someone brought up Sutherland Springs. The presiding bishop admitted that, back before he was a bishop, he had armed security when he was at a church in Chicago.

After the conference, our bishop sent out an e-mail with links to two articles that he called "thoughtful and well-written." The first article said, "True security will come when the people of God care more about life, peace, and justice than they do about losing a few people in their congregations who are holding on more tightly to their guns and their greed than they are to the gospel of Jesus."[1] This did not help me with George.

The second article was less judgmental and more directive. We'd already started to do some of the things it suggested, like meet with police and create security plans. But if a gunman made it inside and started shooting, the article said to "take cover behind a pew, pillar, or balcony."[2] Our church didn't have pews, pillars, or balconies.

The police took us around our building and said we had more "potential projectiles" than any church they had ever assessed: rocks, birdhouses, little glass angels on gravestones. I joked that it was good to be first in something. I was still afraid of George, but he seemed to be OK. He had a job. He had a place to live. He no longer tried to hug me.

* * *

My dad's gun that I had found in the drawer was a 22. After he died, I said to Jan, "We have to do something with his gun."

I considered taking it. After all, if I was going to get a gun, wouldn't my father's gun be the right gun? Even if it was a 22 and wouldn't kill anyone. I didn't want to kill anyone. I thought about it for a few days. I didn't feel safe. I was constantly telling Gary I didn't feel safe.

Dad died on a Tuesday. The funeral was Saturday. The gun was still in the same unlocked drawer. We gave it to my step-nephew after the funeral. His dad was the one who may have taken me shooting when I was ten.

---

[1] Boswell, Benjamin, "Looking for Security at Church? That's What Got Us into This Mess," *Baptist News Global*, November 10, 2017.

[2] Mills, Andrew, "Protect Your Congregation from a Gunman," *CT Pastors*, November 6, 2017.

* * *

After Jan died, Gary gave me a pump shotgun for Christmas. He didn't wrap the gun itself but wrapped up some shotgun buckshot. The wrapped box of buckshot was in the toe of my Christmas stocking. He likes to put the most special gift there. Jewelry, sometimes.

The gun itself was locked away someplace safe. "Before you can hold it or learn how to shoot it," he said, "you have to be able to recite the five safety rules."

"I can't believe you gave me a shotgun," I said. But I could believe it. He was trying to keep me safe.

"You'll never have to use it," he said. "It makes a distinctive sound. If someone breaks in, you just pump it. They'll hear it and leave. Believe me, everybody knows that sound."

* * *

George e-mailed me after Christmas and asked me to call him so he could "say good-bye." To me that sounded suicidal, so I called the police to ask them to do a welfare check, but it turned out he no longer lived at the address we had for him. It turned out he no longer had his job. It also turned out there was a warrant out for his arrest, although the officer said he couldn't tell me what for. Then the officer told me that he had accidentally told George who called them because he thought I had said that I was his sister, not his minister.

I called George. He was mad. We didn't talk long. The police officer also talked to him and kept me posted as they tried to find him. George's mom called too. She told me that George had spent Christmas Eve in jail. I told her George had been at church Christmas Eve. I remembered because he left the service for a few minutes, and I was on high alert. Where had he gone? He came back and I relaxed a little. His mom insisted I was wrong. "That's why he couldn't come to my house," she said. "He was in jail."

Then I remembered the cameras and that our elderly crucifer had her debit card stolen from the sacristy on Christmas Eve. I called someone who knew how the cameras worked, and he met me at the church and found the footage. We could see George go behind the door where the purse was when everyone else was in the service.

I don't know if the police found him. The officer could only tell me a few things. The Sunday that the police couldn't find George,

I felt safer than I ever had. The guys who owned guns handled everything. Gary stood right outside the pulpit and watched the back doors. I preached about prayer. I had never felt so safe. Or loved. Or hypocritical.

George eventually got in touch again, and I told him that I knew he had taken the debit card. I told him that he was not allowed to come back to church until he got a therapist, and I gave him information about where he could get therapy for no cost. I told him his therapist needed to call me so I would know he was getting therapy. Then we could discuss how he could replace the money he had stolen and come up with a plan for getting him back in church safely.

"I am never setting foot in a church again," he said. "Let me go."

In two different Gospels, Jesus talks about the shepherd who leaves ninety-nine sheep to go after the one who was lost. How was I supposed to let George go? What if he called me again to "say goodbye"?

I talked to the church wardens about it. "Let him go," said the senior warden.

I did not become a priest to let people go. I thought about Psalm 23: *surely goodness and mercy shall follow me all the days of my life*. The word translated as "follow" is a stronger word in the Hebrew. "Pursue" would be better. God pursues us with goodness and mercy. I didn't want to give up on George. I wanted a church where he could worship with us and everyone would be safe. George deserves goodness and mercy.

But I let George go. I was afraid of him. I'm still afraid that, somehow, he will read this.

Underneath Quarantine

Because you could be anyone.
And I fall on a dime, let's bore
into quarantine, right through to the other
side, outside and inside "out" spaces.

Let's walk between shadows of ghosts of
crowds, shirking from the touch of points
of ponytails and jacket cuffs, down aisles,
between bookshelves, around dance-floors,

in gazebos above koi ponds. Because I don't
really know you. You could be everyone.
Let's share a kiss in memory of touch
and communion. Let's play Russian Roulette.

I feel lucky. Bet we fall in the uninfected 30 percent.
Because you have a face and fingers and those
are remarkable things. It's already
been so long and some truths hurt. Because still,

honesty. Let's quarantine together, spread
all the good and danger that radiates and
seeps. Let's meet. I'll buy the sake.
We can share a glass.

ANN BRACKEN

Interview with Grace Cavalieri

Even during the pandemic, when most people can't go anywhere, it's tough to get a slot on Grace Cavalieri's dance card. "I'm doing three Zooms today," she told me, when I asked what she'd been up to. "Here I am in my black leather jacket and pajama bottoms, but, really, no one's the wiser."

In some ways, very little has changed for Cavalieri, at least as far as her radio show is concerned. She simply re-routed her recordings with her wonderful engineer Mike Turpin from the Library of Congress site to the sunroom filled with her husband's watercolors at her home in Annapolis. Turpin engineers from afar, and no one can tell the difference. One of her recent video interviews was with Jericho Brown, winner of the 2019 Pulitzer Prize for Poetry for his collection *The Tradition*. Cavalieri had this to say about the interview: "Jericho came right through the algorithms as if he were comfortably in my home. Since we were celebrating Gay Pride Month, he was the perfect candidate for self-actualization."

Photo: Dan Murano

Cavalieri was named poet laureate of Maryland in 2018 by Governor Larry Hogan, and she is in the middle of her four-year term. Like all laureates, she has projects that are designed to shine a light on the value of poetry in modern life. When she was first named to the post, she told me, "I know what I'm going to do. I want to feature all of the wonderful poets in Maryland and put their interviews on the internet. We have so much talent in this state. I'm going to create a state archive. And then I want to work with teens."

"Before the pandemic hit, I was traveling the state and visiting every county to give workshops to interested teens. Do you know what I discovered? One hundred percent of them had never gone inward in their lives. Poetry gave them moments of discovery so they could realize they had an interior life. They discovered that they had enough."

Cavalieri says, "The hardest part of the teen project was

managing all of the logistics. It was quite challenging to find places to meet and record. But I was offering two things that teens love—they love to be seen, and they love to be heard. And my good friend Avideh Shashaani supplied the funding through her organization The Fund for the Future of Children. Her donation has paid for the travel, the engineering, and the uploads. And I'm so grateful."

The long arc of Cavalieri's work displays the talent and dedication for which she is so richly lauded. She's the author of 26 books and chapbooks of poetry and 26 plays, short-form and full-length, produced on American stages. The most recent plays were both performed in New York City: *Anna Nicole: Blonde Glory* in 2012 and *Quilting the Sun* in September 2019.

Cavalieri's latest books are *What the Psychic Said* (Goss Publications, 2020) and *Showboat* (Goss, 2019); *Other Voices, Other Lives*, a compendium of poems, play excerpts, and Library of Congress interviews with poets laureate (Alan Squire Publisher, 2017); *With* (Socomondo Press, 2016); *Life Upon the Wicked Stage: A Memoir* (New Academia/Scarith Press, 2015); *The Mandate of Heaven* (Bordighera Press, 2014); and *The Man Who Got Away* (New Academia, 2014).

The Encyclopedia of Broadcasting celebrated Cavalieri's 44 years of being on public radio as founder of *The Poet and The Poem*, recorded at the Library of Congress, the longest-running poetry series in the history of broadcasting. She has presented approximately 3,000 poets, including all US poets laureate. The series is archived at George Washington University's Gelman Library Special Collections, along with the Pacifica Archives, the Library of Congress, Harvard's *Listening Post*, and University of California, Riverside.

Cavalieri's awards are numerous and impressive, including the 2015 Lifetime Achievement Award from "Books Alive!" with the *Washington Independent Review of Books*. She received the George Garrett Award from the National Associated Writing Program for Outstanding Community Service to Literature, helping the next generation of writers find their way as artists and literary professionals.

In addition to the Dolores Kendrick Poet Laureate Award, the Patterson Center Poetry Award, Humanist of the Year (DC Humanities Council), and the Dragonfly Press Award, she has been honored by the National Commission on Working Women with its highest recognition and the American Association of University Women, among many others.

Cavalieri has four children, four grandchildren, and a great grandchild with her late husband, metal sculptor Kenneth Flynn. She lives and works in Annapolis, MD.

Little Patuxent Review: You've had a long and enduring presence on the radio with your show, *The Poet and the Poem*, for more than 40 years. What is your earliest memory of radio and when did you decide you had to be on the air?

Grace Cavalieri: I love this memory. My first experience of actually being on the radio came through WBUD—the Morrisville, PA, station—across the river from Trenton, NJ, where I grew up. They cast me in a children's show fashioned after the nationally syndicated show *Let's Pretend*. I was a child actor, and, oh, I hated to go home. I remember that we created the sound effect for footsteps in the leaves by rattling paper. Then in college WBUD had an all-night slot for a DJ—how I wanted that—but my dad said I could not be alone in a studio all night. Jean Shepherd's father didn't stop *him*! For 22 years (starting in 1955), Jean Shepherd, an all-night "DJ" from the Midwest, was a storyteller and humorist who became an icon for his radio art. In 1975, I finally bought myself a five-inch reel-to-reel tape recorder. I didn't know where it'd take me, but I wanted to feel the way I did when I was seven.

But when I look back on all of those experiences, I realize that many of them acted as walls that I had to scale in order to achieve my dreams. It's as if my antennae were always up, searching for something better. Everything you want, you have to work to get. My shot at radio came in 1975 when I heard about the new DC radio station WPFW. It got the last spot on the spectrum at that time, so it was hard-won. I went there with my idea of a jazz and literature show and raised money for two years—including obtaining a grant from the National Endowment for the Arts.

I gathered a group of about ten African American artists to work with me in bringing poetry to the airwaves. One of the first poets who performed on my show was Fareedah Allah. She worked as a high school math teacher in DC and was also a jazz musician—I wanted jazz underneath the poetry. Eventually her CDs gained wide acclaim over in Sweden—music really travels. Another poet who performed that first year was Wilfred Cartey, one of the Negritude poets from Trinidad. He was blind and the last living person from that auspicious group of writers. E. Ethelbert Miller was one of the first poets to do a reading, and I had Dolores Kendrick on my show a number of times.

I just love being on the radio and being with other writers and musicians. I love being able to talk to 200 people in a lecture hall, but it's even more wonderful to reach 2,000 people through radio. Many times I've interviewed poets, and we've both been so moved that we were in tears. I've interviewed hundreds of poets. And I've had a most prosperous life.

LPR: Krista Tippett, the host of a podcast called *On Being*, always asks her guests about the spiritual and religious background of their childhood. How would you answer that question?

GC: I was raised Catholic, and I wouldn't trade that for the world. All that incense, all that fainting in church from fear or ecstasy, my Virgin Mary statue in my bedroom. Perfect for a hyperactive imagination. Now I am a Buddhist. It's much more relaxing. But I'm a theist-Buddhist—I make that distinction because not all Buddhists believe in God. Buddhism is low-key and grounding, but I like to soar with the invisible as well.

Catholicism is about possibility, and Buddhism is about daily practice. One of the precepts is "nothing pure, nothing stained." The way I interpret that is that life all boils down to equilibrium. Stillness is good enough. Noticing every moment is the gift Buddhism gives me. I've become so mindful, so healthy. You know, you'll never cut your finger in the kitchen if you're mindful.

LPR: Last year one of your plays, *Quilting the Sun*, was produced by a small theater in New York. How did you come across the story of Harriet Powers, and what inspired you to write the play?

GC: I was commissioned by the Smithsonian Institution and Visual Films (U of MD) to research Harriet's life and write a play for TV. Funding from PBS fell through, so I converted the script from screen to stage. Her quilt hangs in the Smithsonian. That play was all about love. The story of Harriet Powers was found in an old box filled with yellowed papers in the courthouse in Athens, Georgia. There were records about her husband and land and such, but I had to invent a reason for her to sell her quilt to a white woman. So I decided that the only reason she would sell something she worked on for years was to save her son—trading one precious thing for another.

She healed people with Black [folk] medicine, but to heal her son she needed a white doctor. She probably also healed her son, but she needed money to pay the doctor. Harriet's quilts were unique because she told stories and hid messages for runaway enslaved people in them, rather than follow symmetrical, prescribed quilt patterns. One line that I wrote for her is this: "When you do that, I feel like I'm wearing a stone dress."

LPR: Several of your poetry books and plays delve into the lives of famous, iconic women—Mary Wollstonecraft and Anna Nicole Smith come to mind. What drew you to them and how do their lives speak to us today?

GC: They chose me; I didn't choose them. As Sterling Brown said of Ma Rainey, "They jus got ahold of me some kinda way." Mary Wollstonecraft, Harriet Powers, and Anna Nicole Smith each had to fight to be taken seriously. Some never made it. But my plays vindicated each one. I changed the narrative ending for them.

    Anna Nicole was especially in need of vindication. She was completely controlled by ruthless men. She worked in a heartless industry and had no allies whatsoever. All the men around her made her into a fool and a laughingstock. Anna Nicole had no choices—a woman with no choices is not a good thing.

LPR: Governor Hogan appointed you as poet laureate of Maryland in 2018. Two projects that you are working on in that capacity are interviewing Maryland poets for your radio show, *The Poet and the Poem*, and offering poetry workshops for teens across the state. What have been some of the surprising things you've learned doing that work?

GC: My longtime radio show, *The Poet and the Poem*, now incorporates Maryland poets folded within the series as a part of the larger broadcast. If you want to find them as a discrete group, however, they are represented on podcasts under the umbrella *Voices of Maryland Poets*. I know this series could go on forever without ever leaving the state—a pantheon of fabulous writers here. I'm struggling to catch them in my net. And the teen workshops told me young people want to be seen and heard. And want someone to help them look within.

LPR: Anyone who follows you on Facebook has been treated to your foray into painting during the pandemic. What moved you to work with a new medium? What challenged you?

GC: The poet A. R. Ammons once said, "If you are nothing, you can say and do anything." I had the credentials, and it's fun to play in color. I found a blank canvas in Ken's old studio and brought it up to my sunroom. I'm using colors like words, and I just love it. I sat down one day and painted for ten hours and didn't know it. I've done thirty paintings—all gifts for my friends. I have no ego in this project. I'm just having fun and don't want to be constrained by anyone's judgments or standards. The paintings are my way of saying "I love you" in color.

LPR: Tell me more about A. R. Ammons.

GC: He was a fearless poet, and I read him during the cultural revolution in about 1968. He once wrote a whole collection of poems on cash register tape, and he called it *Tape for the Turn of the Year*. He wrote another collection and called it *Garbage*—trying to bait his critics. When I read him, I was ready to fly, and he told me I could. I didn't meet him until his later years.

LPR: How has your life changed during the pandemic? What are some of the ways you've stayed connected with friends and writers?

GC: I teach workshops on Zoom, and I'm on so much I don't think I even need a TV anymore. The visual part is off-putting though, like combing my hair. That's why I like radio. I miss the Library of Congress so much. You know, I love sitting across from my poets and really tapping into their energy. But all of that driving time has been turned over into painting time. So I'm able to make personal cards for people. If you give the paintings as gifts, people will want them. They long for something that's nontransactional.

LPR: I imagine that your listeners feel as if they are sitting in a cozy room with you, sharing a cup of tea, while you talk with poets on your show. What is magical about the human voice?

GC: The voice is the breath of God. The Latin derivation of *voice* and *spirit* are nearly the same. What we say comes from the heart. If you think about it, everything we say is said to elicit something, a sort of spiritual currency. Two people talking to each other communicate values. And when I think of voices, I think of what a very happy life I have.

LPR: I know you wrote the poem "Beyond Its Possibilities" after your husband, Ken, died. But these lines are especially relevant today, with so many people struggling with feelings of isolation and despair. "Loneliness is not exactly solitude. Solitude is not loneliness, as each presses forward into today."

GC: Well, we can be lonely in a crowd of people if we're not with those of a like consciousness. And when we are alone with our art, we're always with "like consciousness." I was terrified to be without him. I was amazed that I could still walk and talk. Then I realized that poetry was my secret lover. And Ken approves of that. I married him when I was 20 and still in college. He was always the principal guiding force in my life, and when he died, I could really appreciate that his financial support allowed me to play in the sandbox [of art and poetry] without pay. And when he was gone, I was left with the legacy that he'd supported.

LPR: In several of your poetry workshops, I've heard you talk about the need for a poem to visit the four quadrants of your Jungian cycle: thinking, feeling, sensual, intuitive. Can you expand on that idea?

GC: Thank you for remembering these important elements of life (and art). Most people start writing with thinking, and the least important is the news report. Imagery and sound are necessary for the sensory; feeling is by word choice (diction) and not outright declaration. Intuition is the hardest, knowing what to leave out, trusting the reader.

LPR: I've attended a few workshops of yours where you take the group into a visualization that you call the elevator of your life. Can you explain how this works and why people find it so valuable?

GC: A spiritual leader once compared our lives to buildings where, at the end of life, the building would crumble. Then I realized that there are many floors in our building, and each year may represent a floor, and if we just get on that elevator and stop at various floors we will find stories; in that way, we're never without material for a poem. This exercise has served me well, and I've never met a beginning poet who couldn't be summoned using this simple way to access their inner world.

LPR: For all the time I've known you, I've seen you put out a book a year. What is your writing process now, and what are you working on?

GC: I am fighting with Madame De Stael, an 18th-century writer who was so great, and Napoleon's biggest enemy. I talked to a psychic today to ask why I could not get her, and Mme. De Stael said, "I don't care." Hah! Anna Nicole and Harriet Powers and Mary Wollstonecraft needed me, but this iceberg does not CARE? Then she said she'd "dip her toe in"—so I may yet get it off the ground. She said to keep fresh flowers on my desk if I want to write about her. What's a writer to do with such a diva?

LPR: In an interview I read with the poet Kathi Wolfe, you said, "Positive attracts negative, and the negative is always going to come in for you to overcome." Can you expand on that?

GC: It's physics, I think. Or magnets. Don't you know when you are riding high, you get a flat tire? Or when you get good news, the bad phone call comes? Life is a balance, and we stand ready to say BRING IT ON. You can't hold back light.

LPR: Finally, what is the role for poets at this time in our history?

GC: The deepest truth inside ourselves is the biggest truth in the universe. We don't have to look any place but inside to our secrets—bring it out, and change the world. POEM BY POEM. Poetry is spirit.

How A Poem Begins

It's a little thing.
Could be the long O's
in Kosovo, or
a woman
alone in the street
after the hurricane
sweeping Honduras.
Perhaps we tell
of the child
beneath the flood
in New Orleans,
or feet bloody
from walking
the rubble of
Afghanistan.
Such a tiny voice
No one can hear.
Sometimes it says
"I can't breathe."
That's why we write
of such little things,
insignificant things.

This Poem Is Asking for Your Love

This poem is not usually like this
I don't know what came over it
It's mostly violet under the sun
with a large yellow parasol and a pond
with a center that never freezes
I swear I had no idea
I'm so used to trees of hearts and
cherries within its branches
I can't imagine
what woke this poem up
with a truth I never wanted
It called out the tower window and said
I was alone
That in itself is a morbid lie
I have long shadows in autumn and clouds
anytime there is a sky
In fact everything was going so well until
this poem wanted to undress me
and bring back my love
and hold me close and rub
my forehead when I had fever
It had no idea what trouble could come
from this so I wrote it
then I ran from it
now I can erase it
to show I never needed it after all
because don't you know, Poem,
if you have to ask for something
it's no gift.

GRACE CAVALIERI

Safety

For Ken Flynn

When you were in the 9th grade and I was in the 7th, you were
a crossing guard keeping order at Junior High School number 3.
    No one
was disobedient when you wore that wide yellow strap across
    your chest—
no one bruised another, caused trouble, or so much as threw a
    stone—
no one cracked a joke about you, a man in uniform. How did
that yellow vest feed your soul to let you know someday you'd
fly a plane just to feel the power of a strap across your chest.
    What
liberation— to know how to be in charge— strong and capable—
flying through gunfire and lightning again and again to come
    back to me.
Although we were young, you were 15 and I was 13, since then,
    I've never
known the world without you. Now I must be 12.

Tomato Pies, 25 Cents

Tomato pies are what we called them, those days,
before Pizza came in,
at my Grandmother's restaurant,
in Trenton New Jersey.
My grandfather is rolling meatballs
in the back. He studied to be a priest in Sicily but
saved his sister Maggie from marrying a bad guy
by coming to America.
Uncle Joey is rolling dough and spooning sauce.
Uncle Joey, is always scrubbed clean,
sobered up, in a white starched shirt, after
cops delivered him home just hours before.
The waitresses are helping
themselves to handfuls of cash out of the drawer,
playing the numbers with Moon Mullin
and Shad, sent in from Broad Street. 1942,
tomato pies with cheese, 25 cents.
With anchovies, large, 50 cents.
A whole dinner is 60 cents (before 6 pm).
How the soldiers, bussed in from Fort Dix,
would stand outside all the way down Warren Street,
waiting for this new taste treat,
young guys in uniform,
lined up and laughing, learning Italian,
before being shipped out to fight the last great war.

Haberdashery

I wish I hadn't made fun of him that day at Union Station when he walked away from the tie rack with the same green and blue striped tie he had in his closet at home. Green and blue slanted stripes. "You have one," I laughed. He said maybe the stripes are wider on the other one. I proved I was right. They were identical. I proved it. "Why have two exactly alike?" *Because I like that tie*, he said. *I always liked this tie.* Then I recalled when I was 17 and his mother took the hat right off my head. She liked it. Actually my father did this when she said, *Isn't that adorable*. He took it right off my head and handed it to her. I never found another. None of this is what I want to talk about. This second, I want to show you the way the sun lights up the tree, such a funny slice of light, it couldn't be made by design, the way it hits the angle of green. There will never be another moment like it.

KAREN KORETSKY

Supermoon

I kneel on a grassy hillside in Arlington, Massachusetts, on a windy October evening at twilight. My dog, Chloe, is pressed to my side as she does—my constant companion. The sun moves toward the horizon behind me, leaving trails of glowing striations: orange, pink, and purple. I take a photo of the sunset, and then I turn to gaze in the opposite direction. Gathered around me are dozens of strangers, united by anticipation. We are here for the same reason: to watch a supermoon rise. It is getting chilly, and I am thankful for my warm fleece jacket. I yank up the zipper and rub my hands together to generate some heat. I coax Chloe onto my lap, and she warms my legs although she is shivering a little too. The ground is cold, hard, and uneven. People around me seem more comfortable. They recline on picnic blankets or sit in camping chairs. It is a lunar celebration to witness celestial light in a sea of night. My fellow observers munch on chips or drink tea from thermoses while they watch the slow ascension of the moon.

There are lovers here, young couples with children, old couples, and even some sort of meditation group that is ringing Tibetan bowls and chanting. The mournful sound of a flute rides the air like a wail. Waves of melancholy flood my mind: how sad I am to be alone and not snuggled up to a lover, sharing body warmth and a future. But I am used to this situation. I am midlife and in the second year of my separation; my children are in college. I am almost divorced. Even though my days are edged with loneliness and uncertainty, research assures me that I am in good company. I have read that Americans over 50 are twice as likely to get divorced as people that age were 20 years ago. That means one in four couples over the age of 50 are getting divorced, a trend referred to as the "graying" of divorce. While these statistics do not resolve my loneliness, I know somewhere out there someone just like me is watching a supermoon and wishing they had someone to share it with. My anticipation of finding a new partner is sometimes all-consuming. It may never happen. So I purposefully set out to find human connection; I don't want to rise alone like the moon.

One of the unique features of my suburban town outside of Boston is the topography. The Arlington elevation ranges from a low of 4 feet to high of 377 feet. The highest point in town is a place called Robbins Farm, which used to be a working farm more than a hundred years ago. Now it is a playground, field, and recreation space.

But on nights like this, Robbins Farm is an enchanting place with a near panoramic view of the sky and shimmering views of the cityscapes of Cambridge, Boston, and the southern suburbs. There is even a glimpse of Boston Harbor. It is the perfect place to watch the moon.

 Decades ago, on a July evening, I came to this hill with a man I was dating. We had a few beers and stretched out on a beach blanket to watch the summer Perseid meteor shower. I was so enamored by Gregory; I loved his height, his intelligence, and his charm. A few weeks later, we broke up. I think of Gregory as I sit here tonight and wonder what ever happened to him. My love life has been meteor-like: bright hopeful bursts that leave me in awe, followed by a rapid descent and loss. At times I have visited Robbins Farm and imagined I am a bird soaring through the air or an ancient empress scanning my kingdom from a tower on a hill. It's hard not to feel that kind of wonder and freedom here.

 The moon appears through the craggy branches of a cluster of oak trees. Slowly she rises, plump and radiant like a pregnant goddess. Her ascension seems aligned to my slow, even breath, and with each exhale she climbs a bit higher in the sky. My fellow moon watchers exclaim, point, and snap photos of the glorious golden disk smiling down upon us. Eventually the sky darkens, and I decide to return to my car and drive home in pools of moonlight. Chloe lies down on the passenger seat and sighs.

 I remember the times when I was a child, sitting in the back of my parents' Dodge Dart, coming home from a road trip when the moon seemed to follow me, chasing the car along long stretches of highway. Mother moon lights my way, and I although I am headed home to an empty house I don't feel lonely. Perhaps being among so many people gave me a sense of connection.

Communal Rest

The next morning, I force myself out into the chilly morning air to walk to a yoga class. The meditative parts of the class seem to overflow into my non-yoga days to help me feel centered. I hope that it will help me sleep tonight. The community room where the yoga takes place is dusty and grand. It has a vaulted ceiling with exposed wood beams. Medieval-looking wrought iron lanterns dangle precariously from rusty links and distract me when I gaze up. The room is lined with tall sixteen-paned windows that offer generous glimpses of sky, birds in trees, and leaves rustling in the wind. I leave my judgment of my body at the door. The thighs too plump to squeeze into my jeans from last summer are strong, reliable supports during extended lunge poses—like a tree trunk supporting the growth of a tree. There are no mirrors here, and I cannot fixate on the appearance of my shape. Rather, the yoga teacher talks about the journey of yoga, the joining of body, mind, and spirit. She speaks of hearts opening and talks of the universe as a benevolent goddess. I concentrate on my movement and thank a body that complies, exhausts, and relaxes.

In yoga class, I am in a community of movement and mindfulness. During our final pose, Shavasana, I lie on my back and allow the floor to support me. I open my palms to the ceiling, ready to accept blessings from above. I feel the energy of the room full of people. We are resting together. I realize that these are the only people I lie with now. The floor creaks with the subtle movements of the others in the class settling. I hear their breath, someone clears their throat, another is softly snoring. It is comforting. I hear the teacher's footsteps, lightly moving throughout the room. Then she is close to me. She smells like lavender. She tucks the yoga blanket I've draped over myself around my feet and gives my toes a gentle squeeze. She slips her palms under my shoulder blades and lifts them. She removes her hands and applies gentle pressure on my shoulders. I hear her knee or toe crack. I am alone and not alone. In this community of movement, I maintain connection so I don't drown in the longing.

The Sensations

In the afternoon, I am waiting for the dentist and filled with dread. I need a cavity drilled. The dental assistant cheerfully clips a crinkly paper around my neck and reclines my chair. Then she leaves. Alone in this room, not distracted enough by the pop music coming from a speaker in the ceiling, I become apprehensive. I stare at the ceiling; I do not like being confined, unable to spring up and run. I hear cars whiz by, the people outside this office on their way somewhere, but I am prone, powerless. Suspended in time and space. I would rather be anywhere but here. I hear the annoying plunk plunk of a slow drip from the faucet into the metal sink. The dentist comes in, smelling of antiseptic, asks about my life and children with a sincere concern in her voice. She speaks with a soft, slow cadence, a charming hint of a lisp. She gazes at me through thick protective glasses. She looks directly into my eyes, then with a whoosh of her rolling stool her voice moves to somewhere behind my head. I hear drawers open and close, metal instruments clink. I know she is preparing my Novocain injection. With a whoosh, she is back beside me. Wearing rubber gloves, she grasps my jawline and turns my face toward hers. She gently rubs my lower left jawbone with one hand while she injects the upper left side of my mouth. I barely notice the pain of the needle plunging into the soft doughy flesh of my gums because of the tenderness of her touch.

Twenty years ago, I was in the waiting room of a salon, scheduled for a facial. My esthetician emerged and escorted a woman with wiry white hair and a cane to the door.

"Does *she* get facials?" I asked.

"No. She lives around the corner and comes in once a week for a back rub," the esthetician replied.

"A backrub? Why?"

"Because she has no one in her life, and it is the only time she is touched."

I had a hard time wrapping my mind around paying for touch. I had small kids at home, I was teaching children at the time, and I longed for time alone and to *not* be touched.

Now I am one step closer to becoming the old woman who pays for a back rub, and I am ashamed I didn't have more compassion then.

I've heard other middle-aged women complain about this sort of invisible cloak that covers us. In a culture where youth and beauty are revered, those of us aging and losing some of our outer glow often go unnoticed.

"I am sorry," the dentist apologizes once she has withdrawn the needle. Numbness slowly spreads throughout my mouth, lips, and nose. I forget the pain in a flash for a fleeting second just because I am being attended to. What ensues are the noises of a drill, vibration in my mouth and ears, a blinding light in my face, cotton wads shoved in my lip pocket, a suction wand that leaves my mouth parched, and a jet stream of water to cool the heated and drilled tooth. The sensations are overwhelming—but they are sensations, after all.

The Universe

I try to trust the universe. I believed that by taking a leap of faith, leaving a miserable marriage, and deciding to live alone, I might find true love. Now I am discovering how to love myself. A hard and unexpected lesson. One can be single and feel connected. And this is where I am, at midlife trying to re-create a life, and it isn't easy. My younger self clearly imagined middle-aged me, settled and comfortable: "settled" being synonymous with love, partnership, and being happy. Instead, I am wrestling with something unexpected and unwieldly: a divorce and all its accoutrements of self-doubt, aloneness, insecurity, and fear. But beyond those unsteady emotions also exists the strength I receive from facing self-doubt, aloneness, insecurity, and fear. I may not have a lover, someone who adores me. But I *am* surrounded by love and light. Just like the moonrise or in yoga class, I try to notice.

Just like the moon, I rise and fall. Somedays I radiate the assurance and comfort of a single being, and other days I long to shrink away in a pool of darkness. I have learned to be among many and have no one.

ROBERT L. PENICK

Duty

He was sixty-three years old
before he got it right, before
he left off missing being missed
or loved or wanted, and got on with
the rituals that would become
his life. Days moved like a carousel,
each dawn that bright yellow horse
passing by again.

This is what you have left
the walls told him, and he took
the hours and joined them together
until he had something to show
that damned bright steed.

And so he remains,
punctual to his habits and mission
until his heart and the sun
burn themselves out.

SUSAN JOHNSON

Crumbs

A woman walks by a famous
poet's house, dark & empty,
except for the mice searching
for crumbs: of manuscripts,
of the poet's award-winning
bread. What are you after?
ask the mice. Crumbs of her
imagination, says the woman.
Isn't that what everyone wants?
To see what her window sees.
Below the poet's window,
the sidewalk is shoveled
but still icy. Always those
patches to watch out for.
So that's what the street
lights do. Watch. We got
this, they tell the woman.
You can proceed without
risk. At night, in winter,
teeth are at their sharpest,
she says. Risk is what
it's all about. Risk &
stealth, say the mice.
& feathers, says the poet.

Contributors' Notes
WINTER 2021

Abdu Mongo Ali is an American avant-garde musician, writer, cultural worker, and multidisciplinary artist. Their music is an idiosyncratic blend of punk, jazz, Baltimore club music, and rap that has graced stages across the U.S. and Europe.

Mischelle Anthony's poems lately appear or are forthcoming in *Cimarron Review*, *I-70 Review*, *Cream City Review*, *Ocean State Review*, *American Chordata*, and in her collection *[Line]* (Foothills Press). She edited an 1807 memoir of sexual assault, *Lucinda; Or, The Mountain Mourner* (Syracuse University Press). She lives and works in Wilkes-Barre, Pennsylvania.

Brian Wallace Baker holds an MFA from Western Kentucky University. His book reviews, interviews, and creative work have appeared in *Atticus Review*, *Colorado Review*, *Split Lip Magazine*, *River Teeth*, *Poets Reading the News*, and elsewhere.

David Bergman is the author of four books of poetry. The most recent one is *Fortunate Light* (2013). *Cracking the Code* was the winner of the George Elliston Poetry Prize. His critical books include *The Poetry of Disturbance* and *Gaiety Transfigured*. He edited John Ashbery's art chronicles *Reported Sightings* and Edmund White's *The Burning Library*. His poetry has appeared in the *Kenyon Review*, the *Yale Review*, Poetry, the *Paris Review*, and many other publications.

Ann Bracken, an activist with a pen, has written two poetry collections, *No Barking in the Hallways: Poems from the Classroom* and *The Altar of Innocence*; is a contributing editor for *Little Patuxent Review*; and cofacilitates the Wilde Readings Poetry Series in Columbia, Maryland. Her poetry, essays, and interviews have appeared in anthologies and journals, including *Bared: Contemporary Poetry & Art on Bras & Breasts*, *Fledgling Rag*, *Gargoyle*, and *ArLiJo*. Ann's poetry has garnered two Pushcart Prize nominations. She offers writing workshops in school at conferences, and in community education centers. Her advocacy work centers on arts-based interventions for education, mental health, and prison reform.

Grace Cavalieri is Maryland's tenth Poet Laureate. She's the author of 26 books and chapbooks of poetry and 20 short-form and full-length plays. *What The Psychic Said* is her new publication (Goss

Publications, 2020.) The previous book of poems is *Showboat*, (Goss publications 2019,) about 25 years as a Navy wife. Her latest play "Quilting The Sun" was produced at the Theater for the New City, NYC in 2019. She founded and produces "the Poet and the Poem" for public radio, now from the Library of Congress, celebrating 44 years on-air.

Catherine-Esther Cowie is from the Caribbean island of St. Lucia and has lived in Canada and the United States. She is a graduate of Pacific University's low-residency MFA program. Her writing has appeared in the *Penn Review*, *Glass: A Journal of Poetry*, *Forklift Ohio*, *Flock Literary Journal*, *Moko Magazine*, *The Common*, *Potomac Review*, *Southern Humanities Review*, and *Portland Review*.

Alyssa Cruz is a Filipina American poet, born and raised in the suburbs of the Pacific Northwest. Her work has appeared in *Bricolage Journal* and the *Atlanta Review*. In 2018, Alyssa was awarded the Dan Veach Prize for Younger Poets. She currently lives in Seattle with her puppy, Berkeley.

Madison Durand is a junior in high school who loves to tell stories. She's passionate about creating work that compels, provokes, and challenges readers to question the conditions of the human spirit. Her short stories have been recognized multiple times by the Association of Christian Schools International, where she recently obtained a superior rating for her piece *Eliot*. She also enjoys watching old films and spending time with her family and her poodle.

Elizabeth Felicetti is a writer and Episcopal priest. Her creative essays have been published in *Modern Loss*, *Christian Century*, *Entropy*, the *Other Journal*, the *Grief Diaries*, and others, and her academic essays have appeared in Westminster John Knox's Connections series. Check out her poetry in *Waterways*, *Barren Magazine*, and the anthology *Lingering on the Margins*. She holds an MFA from Spalding School of Writing and tweets @bizfel.

Pete Fortenbaugh is 30 years old and from Maryland's Eastern Shore. He has been writing stories about the fictional Chesapeake island of Johnsontown for nearly 10 years. His first book, a 91-page novella entitled *Charles Thomas's Monday after Father's Day or Revelations: A Parable*, is due to be published in early spring 2021 by Head to Wind Publishing.

Susan Thornton Hobby is a former newspaper journalist with a master's in literature. A 25-year board member of the Howard County Poetry and Literature Society, Hobby is also an artistic advisor and produces their television shows. As a founding member of the *Little Patuxent Review*, Hobby interviews authors for publication. As an editor, Hobby has prepared dozens of manuscripts for publication, including collections and anthologies of poetry and nonfiction about sports and history. She also writes fiction—in her Ellicott City garden if she's lucky.

Liz Holland is an MFA candidate at the University of Baltimore. Her work can be found in *Marias at Sampaguitas*, *The Kraken Spire*, and is forthcoming in the *Remington Review* and *Broadkill Review*.

Susan Johnson received her MFA and PhD from the University of Massachusetts Amherst, where she currently teaches writing. Her poems have recently appeared in *North American Review*, *San Pedro River Review*, *Trampoline*, *Steam Ticket*, *Front Range*, and *SLAB*. She lives in South Hadley, Massachusetts.

Kristin Kowalski Ferragut writes, teaches, plays guitar, hikes, supports her children in becoming who they are meant to be, and enjoys the vibrant writing community in the DC-Maryland-Virginia area. Her work has appeared in *Beltway Quarterly*, *Nightingale and Sparrow*, *Bourgeon*, *Magnolia Review*, *Mojave He[Art] Review*, *Anti-Heroin Chic*, and *Fledgling Rag*, among others. Kristin's poetry collection *Escape Velocity* will be released by Kelsay Books in April 2021.

Karen Koretsky is a writer, visual artist, and arts advocate, living in Massachusetts. Her work has been published in the *Boston Globe*, *Spirit of Change Magazine*, *Health Magazine*, *Phoebe*, *Alternating Current*, *Writer's Rock*, and *Iris Literary Review*. She received her MFA in creative writing from the Solstice Program of Pine Manor College and is crafting a memoir. Her website is: www.karenkoretsky.com.

Briana Maley's short stories have been published in *Fiction Southeast*, *New Flash Fiction Review*, *Cagibi*, *Literary Mama*, and elsewhere. She received *Lilith Magazine*'s 2019 fiction prize and was runner-up in the 2020 F. Scott Fitzgerald Literary Festival fiction contest. She lives in Maryland.

Jihoon Park's fiction is forthcoming or published in *Spry Literary Journal, No Contact Magazine, Mary: A Journal of New Writing*, and elsewhere. He is currently a MFA candidate at George Mason University in Northern Virginia.

Robert L. Penick's poetry and prose have appeared in more than 100 different literary journals, including *The Hudson Review, North American Review,* and *The California Quarterly*. His latest book is *Exit, Stage Left*, from Slipstream Press. More of his work can be found at theartofmercy.net.

Rachele Salvini is from Italy but is currently based in the United States, where she's working toward her PhD in English and creative writing at Oklahoma State University. Her work in English has been published or is forthcoming in *Takahe Magazine, Prime Number, American Book Review, Bull, Necessary Fiction*, and others.

s.e.a. is a photographer and artist whose work explores love, joy, intimacy, vulnerability, kink, sex and sexuality, identity, and movement within the confines of our *human* bodies, specifically Queer Black and Brown bodies. She strives to push boundaries that are placed on us, that we place on ourselves, and others, while trying to always find and capture moments of beauty. Born and raised on St. Croix, U.S.V.I., she lives and works in Brooklyn, New York. More of her work can be found at www.sea-foto.net.

Mary Beth Stuller is a high school English teacher who lives in Parkton, Maryland, where she tends chickens and dreams of being a flower farmer. She is pursuing an MA in fiction writing at Johns Hopkins University.

Sarah B. Sullivan, of Northampton, Massachusetts, has three self-published chapbooks: *While It Happened*; *Together, in Pieces*; and *Somewhere There Is Always Enough*. She is published in several journals, including *Cider Press Review, Switchgrass Review, Sixfold, Wordpeace, FreeLit Magazine,* and *Western Massachusetts Medical Magazine*. She is currently enrolled at Pacific University in the Masters of Fine Arts program in poetry. Her website is sarahbsullivan.com.

Sophia Tarin is a writer and educator. Her poetry has been published in *New Square, Prometheus Dreaming, So to Speak*, and The Rainbow Poems' anthology *Sonnets for Shakespeare*. A Long Island native, she is an adjunct professor of English at Adelphi University where she is currently an MFA candidate in creative writing. She is currently on the staff of the Walt Whitman Birthplace Assocation.

Elyse Thomas is a 17-year-old, second-generation Puerto Rican and Jamaican writer from Miami, Florida. She has been recognized by The Poetry Society, Alliance for Young Writers, the Poetry Society of Virginia, It's All Write, the National English Honor Society, and Just Poetry. Her work is published or forthcoming in *Foyle Young Poets*, *The Poetry Society of Virginia*, *The Bridge Bluffton University Literary Journal*, *Polyphony Lit*, *Gyroscope Review*, *Alexandria Quarterly*, and more.

Kathleen Wheaton grew up in California and studied at Stanford University. She worked as a freelance journalist in Spain, Argentina, Brazil, Mexico, and Bethesda and now interprets Spanish and Portuguese for Montgomery County Public Schools. Her fiction has appeared in many journals and three anthologies, and she is a five-time recipient of Maryland State Arts Council grants. Her collection *Aliens and Other Stories* won the Washington Writers Publishing House Fiction Prize.

Evan Williams is an undergraduate at the University of Chicago, where he thinks about family, masculinity, and surrealism. His poems have appeared or are forthcoming in the *Rockvale Review*, *Rogue Agent Journal*, and *Diagram*, among others.

In the Next Issue...

Little Patuxent Review will be seeking submissions of poetry, fiction, nonfiction, and visual art for its Summer 2021 issue. The issue is unthemed, so write with abandon, occupy your imagination, and send *LPR* your best writing.

Prose submissions should be no longer than 5,000 words for fiction and 3,500 words for nonfiction. Submit up to three poems of any style; 100-line limit. Submissions may be uploaded at Submittable, littlepatuxentreview.submittable.com/submit. Please note that *Little Patuxent Review* does not accept hard-copy submissions. Visual artists are invited to submit up to six images for consideration. Images can be submitted via e-mail to editor@littlepatuxentreview.org and should be no larger than 5 MB in JPEG or TIFF format.

Published authors will receive one copy of the *Review* in payment.

THE READING PERIOD FOR SUBMISSIONS IS DECEMBER 1, 2020—MARCH 1, 2021.

SUBSCRIBE TO LITTLE PATUXENT REVIEW

Subscribe online at littlepatuxentreview.org or
send a check payable to *Little Patuxent Review* for $20 to:
Little Patuxent Review
P.O. Box 6084
Columbia, MD 21045
Attention: Subscriptions

ONE YEAR (TWO ISSUES) $20

Printed by our sponsor

indigoink
DIGITAL PRINTING
WWW.INDIGOINKPRINT.COM